Words of Victory

...the Prevailing Word!

Books by Author

Travel Through Ephesians (2013)

Travel Through The Old Testament Vol. 1 (2016)

Travel Through The Old Testament Vol. 2 (2017)

God's Armor Against Satan's Weapons (2018)

(Tom Hiegel Bible Study Series, #1)

Book of Old Testament Bible Literacy (2018)

Help from the Bible...When you need it!

Words of Victory

...the Prevailing Word!

THOMAS L. HIEGEL

Table of Contents

ABBREVIATIONS

Old Testament Books

Gen	Genesis	Lam	Lamentations	Acts	Acts
Ex	Exodus	Ezek	Ezekiel	Rom	Romans
Lev	Leviticus	Dan	Daniel	1-2 Cor	1-2 Corinthians
Num	Numbers	Hos	Hosea	Gal	Galatians
Deut	Deuteronomy	Joel	Joel	Eph	Ephesians
Josh	Joshua	Amos	Amos	Phil	Philippians
Judg	Judges	Oba	Obadiah	Col	Colossians
Ruth	Ruth	Jon	Jonah	1-2 Thess	1-2 Thessalonians
1-2 Sam	1-2 Samuel	Mic	Micah	1-2 Tim	1-2 Timothy
1-2 Kings	1-2 Kings	Nah	Nahum	Tit	Titus
1-2 Chron	1-2 Chronicles	Hab	Habakkuk	Phi	Philemon
Ezra	Ezra	Zeph	Zephaniah	Heb	Hebrews
Neh	Nehemiah	Hag	Haggai	Jam	James
Est	Esther	Zech	Zechariah	1-2 Pet	1-2 Peter
Job	Job	Mal	Malachi	1-3 Jn	1-2-3 John
Ps	Psalms			Jude	Jude
Prov	Proverbs	**New Testament Books**		Rev	Revelation
Eccl	Ecclesiastes	Matt	Matthew		
SofS	Song of Songs	Mark	Mark		
Isa	Isaiah	Luke	Luke		
Jer	Jeremiah	John	John		

INTRODUCTION

In 1995, I presented my daughter with a three-ring notebook of Scriptures on many topics I thought would be a blessing for her...Scriptures when she needed them quickly.

Since that time, the original notebook has been close to my desk and referred to hundreds of times. It began when I couldn't fall to sleep at nights. So I looked at what God said about the topic, discovering "He gives His beloved (ME) sleep" and "I will lie down and my sleep will be sweet." So I just received those Words, and have never failed to have a good night's rest!

The original notebook, written out by hand, is still by my desk and is the basis for *Words of Victory...the Prevailing Word*.

HELP! The word that many literally "cry out" when a problem, difficulty, or just a question arises. It's at that time or even that moment, that a Christian wants an answer. Granted, every question or trial does not have a definite answer. However, I have found that there IS a source for immediate assistance with most difficult times. This is the reason for this book you hold in your hand. Become familiar with its contents and refer to the Scriptures for the topic of concern.

So, to introduce you to this "answer book," we note that the entire source of HELP comes from the Bible. The Bible contains the WORDS OF GOD. Those WORDS are filled with His Creative Force. Yes, they were written down by human persons. But the origin of Scripture is divine. The precise mode of inspiration He used to convey His words remains a mystery, but you can trust that the words are His Words.

"In the Beginning God Created..."
He manifested His Creation by speaking forth His Words. He created everything and He controls everything.

We see His pattern over and over again in Genesis, "God said...and it was so," "God said...and it was so." To a believer, the Life contained in HIS WORDS is of vital importance. Many are saved and begin their life with Jesus Christ as a result of first *hearing* the Word of God and then *acting* upon it. I Corinthians tells us we became a new creation instantly (creation-at-work!). Growth and closeness to our Father God develop from the same pattern. We must never stop following this is pattern throughout our life. As we read the Bible, and begin to believe, stand upon, and release those Words in situations of our life, His Creative Power begins to work. It's exciting to know, *even the believing* is created inside the spirit and soul by hearing the Words. (Romans 10:17). Believing is then reinforced with prayer and action.

When problems, difficulties, decisions or goals are before you, allow the Creative Force of God to work with you. I *have released this book based on this theme.* I realize that many Christians desire to know more about the Bible but have little time to study. The scriptures and studies included in this notebook were compiled over many years of ministry. NOTE that many of the Scriptures listed for a topic are NOT a research tool for "in context" interpretation. My desire in this work is to offer the attitude and character of God towards the specific topic. The topics marked "skh" were added by my wife, Sandy.

I hope they will immediately help you and serve as a study tool. Locate the topic from the Contents Page, turn to that alphabetized topic and read over and over what God says.

Read them
Say them
Pray them

Establish your own topics, adding them to your study notes. They will personalize your study for life-long benefit.

There are also a variety of inspirational helps included in this notebook. These helps, along with most of the categorized scriptures and studies, have been collected and/or written by the author over the past 60 years.

These added notes and studies, along with the categories of scriptures, have meant a great deal in *my own* life. Use them for victory in every area of *your* life.

FOUNDATION FOR THIS WORK

Luke 4:4 *And Jesus answered him, "It is written, 'MAN SHALL NOT LIVE ON BREAD ALONE.'"*

Heb 4:12 *For the Word that God speaks is alive and full of power [making it active, operative, energizing, and effective]; it is sharper than any two-edged sword, penetrating to the dividing line of the breath of life (soul) and [the immortal] spirit, and of joints and marrow [of the deepest parts of our nature],*

14

exposing and sifting and analyzing and judging the very thoughts and purposes of the heart. AMP

Jer 1:12 *Then the Lord said to me, "You have seen well, for I am watching over My word to perform it."*

Ps 119:105 *Your word is a lamp to my feet And a light to my path.*

2 Peter 1:4 *For by these He has granted to us His precious and magnificent promises, so that by them you may become partakers of the divine nature...*

1 Peter 4:11... *if someone speaks, let him speak God's words;*

Mark 11:24-25 *Therefore I say to you, all things for which you pray and ask, believe that you have received them, and they will be granted you.*

Josh 1:8-9 *Yes, keep this book of the Torah on your lips, and meditate on it day and night, so that you will take care to act according to everything written in it. Then your undertakings will prosper, and you will succeed.* CJB

Ps 1:2 *But his delight is in the law of the Lord, And in His law he meditates day and night.*

Rev 22:18-19 *I warn everyone hearing the words of the prophecy in this book that if anyone adds to them, God will add to him the plagues written in this book. 19 And if anyone takes anything away from the words in the book of this prophecy, God will take away his share in the Tree of Life and the holy city, as described in this book.* CJB

HOW DO I USE THIS BOOK?

As a result of many asking this question, I offer the following suggestions:

Personal Help for You

1. Locate the topic of need in the Contents, or by the alphabetical pages.
2. Read the suggested verses several times. For example: if you need joy in your life, turn to the page on joy and read the many scriptures over and over.
3. Understand that these are God's Words and accept His statements as being personal.

4. Pray that the Scriptures read are working in your life. Do not accept anything less than what He has said. (The world, the flesh, and the devil will all offer you doubt).

Other Uses for this book

5. Daily personal devotion help.
6. Source of a topic for large or small group studies, classes, and sermons. The author has used this book in notebook form, for hundreds of speaking engagements. Many of these are marked "A STUDY."
7. Instant reference as you are having conversations over the phone.
8. Carry along with your Bible to all gatherings (studies, services, etc.). Use as a reference to help in the study. Add to your notes from these gatherings.

John 15:4 *"Abide in Me, and I in you."*

John 15:7 *"If you abide in Me, and My words abide in you, ask whatever you wish, and it will be done for you."*

John 15:10 *If you keep My commandments, you will abide in My love;*

1 John 2:6 *...the one who says he abides in Him ought himself to walk in the same manner as He walked.*

1 John 2:24 *As for you, let that abide in you which you heard from the beginning. If what you heard from the beginning abides in you, you also will abide in the Son and in the Father.*

1 John 2:28 *Now, little children, abide in Him...*

ABUNDANCE

A STUDY

GOD GIVES US ABUNDANT LIFE THROUGH CHRIST JESUS
Phil 1:26 *...so that through my being with you again your joy in Christ Jesus will overflow on account of me.* NIV

Note that the Apostle John's books are books of life:

John 10:10 *The thief comes only to steal and kill and destroy; I came that they may have life, and have it abundantly.*

John 10:28 *... and I give eternal life to them...*

John 1:4 *"In him was life; and the life was the light of men."*

GOD PROMISES US ABUNDANT HARVEST
Isa 60:5 *Then you shall see and become radiant, And your heart shall swell with joy; Because the abundance of the sea shall be turned to you, The wealth of the Gentiles shall come to you.* NKJV

Deut 33:19 *For they will draw out the abundance of the seas, And the hidden treasures of the sand.*

Isa 35:2 *Yes, there will be an abundance of flowers and singing and joy!*

Acts 2:47 *And the Lord was adding to their number day by day those who were being saved.*

Acts 2:40-41 *So then, those who had received his word were baptized; and that day there were added about three thousand souls.*

Acts 19:18-20 *Many also of those who had believed kept coming, confessing and disclosing their practices. 19 And many of those who practiced magic brought their books together and began burning them in the sight of everyone; and they counted up the price of them and found it fifty thousand pieces of silver. 20 So the word of the Lord was growing mightily and prevailing.*

Rev 7:9 *After these things I looked, and behold, a great multitude which no one could count, from every nation and all tribes and peoples and tongues, standing before the throne and before the Lamb...*

GOD PROMISES ABUNDANCE OF SUCCESS

2 Chron 15:9 *Then he gathered all Judah and Benjamin, and those who dwelt with them...for they came over to him in great numbers from Israel when they saw that the Lord his God was with him.* NKJ

Ps 1:3 *Whatever he does prospers.* NIV

Josh 1:8 *This Book of the Law shall not depart from your mouth, but you shall meditate in it day and night, that you may observe to do according to all that is written in it. For then you will make your way prosperous, and then you will have good success.* NKJV

GOD PROMISES ABUNDANCE OF PEACE AND TRUTH

Ex 34:6 *Then the Lord passed by in front of him and proclaimed, "The Lord, the Lord God, compassionate and gracious, slow to anger, and abounding in lovingkindness and truth;"*

Jer 33: *Behold, I will bring to it health and healing, and I will heal them; and I will reveal to them an abundance of peace and truth.*

Ps 37:11 *But the meek shall inherit the earth, And shall delight themselves in the abundance of peace.* NKJV

GOD PROMISES ABUNDANCE OF GRACE

Rom 5:17 *...those who receive the abundance of grace and of the gift of righteousness will reign in life through the One, Jesus Christ.*

1 Tim 1:14 *...the grace of our Lord was more than abundant, with the faith and love which are found in Christ Jesus.*

GOD PROMISES ABUNDANCE OF PARDON

Isa 55:7 *Let the wicked forsake his way*

And the unrighteous man his thoughts;
And let him return to the Lord,
And He will have compassion on him,
And to our God,
For He will abundantly pardon.

Rom 10:13 *"WHOEVER WILL CALL ON THE NAME OF THE LORD WILL BE SAVED."*

1 John 1:9 *If we confess our sins, He is faithful and righteous to forgive us our sins and to cleanse us from all unrighteousness.*

GOD PROMISES ABUNDANCE OF RICHES AND HONOR

2 Chron 17:5-6 *So the Lord established the kingdom in his control, and all Judah brought tribute to Jehoshaphat, and he had great riches and honor. 6 He took great pride in the ways of the Lord.*

2 Chron 32:29 *He made cities for himself and acquired flocks and herds in abundance, for God had given him very great wealth.*

Josh 22:8-9 *...and said to them, "Return to your tents with great riches and with very much livestock, with silver, gold, bronze, iron, and with very many clothes; divide the spoil of your enemies with your brothers."*

Matt 6:33 *But seek first His kingdom and His righteousness, and all these things will be added to you.*

It was not the intent of this notebook to include any detailed, exhaustive studies on a topic. However, in a few cases, such as this one on ANGELS and others such as the study on SATAN, I found the study so interesting that the entire study is included. For those who are not detail oriented, please skip through the study. For others, I hope it is valuable to you or your group study.

THEY ARE SPIRIT BEINGS
Heb 1:14 *Are not the angels all ministering spirits (servants) sent out in the service [of God for the assistance] of those who are to inherit salvation?* AMP

Luke 20:36 *For they cannot die again, but they are angel-like and equal to angels. And being sons of and sharers in the resurrection, they are sons of God.* "(referring to those resurrected) AMP

THEY WERE CREATED BY GOD (BEFORE MAN AND EARTH)
Ps 148:2-6 *Praise Him, all His angels...5 Let them praise the name of the Lord, for He commanded and they were created. 6 He also established them forever and ever...* AMP

Col 1:16 *For it was in Him that all things were created, in heaven and on earth, things seen and things unseen, whether thrones, dominions, rulers, or authorities; all things were created and exist through Him [by His service, intervention] and in and for Him.* AMP

Job 38:4-7 *Where were you when I laid the foundation of the earth? Declare to Me, if you have and know understanding. 5 Who determined the measures of the earth, if you know? Or who stretched the measuring line upon it? 6 Upon what were the foundations of it fastened, or who laid its cornerstone, 7 When the morning stars sang together and all the sons of God shouted for joy?* AMP

Sons of God in the Old Testament
6 times, each time meaning supernatural beings: Gen 6:2, Job 1:6, 2:1, 38:7, Ps 29:1, 89:6. Each time they are good Angels of God.

ORGANIZATION OF ANGELIC BEINGS

Luke 2:13 *Then suddenly there appeared with the angel an army of the troops of heaven (a heavenly knighthood), praising God and saying...* AMP

Three ruling angels named in the Scriptures

1. GABRIEL Dan 8:15-16 *When I, even I, Daniel, had seen the vision, I sought to understand it; then behold, there stood before me one [Gabriel] with the appearance of a man. 16 And I heard a man's voice between the banks of the [river] Ulai which called and said, Gabriel, make this man [Daniel] understand the vision.* (Also see Dan 9:20-27) AMP

   Luke 1:19 *And the angel replied to him, I am Gabriel* AMP

   Luke 1:26 *Now in the sixth month [after that], the angel Gabriel was sent from God...* AMP

2. MICHAEL Dan 11:1 *I [the angel], in the first year of Darius the Mede, even I, stood up to confirm and to strengthen him [Michael, the angelic prince].* AMP

Dan 10:18-21 Then this one with human appearance touched me again and strengthened me... 21 Yet there is no one who stands firmly with me against these forces except Michael your prince.

Jude 9 But when [even] the archangel Michael, contending with the devil, judicially argued (disputed) about the body of Moses, he dared not [presume to] bring an abusive condemnation against him, but [simply] said, The Lord rebuke you. AMP

3. LUCIFER Isa 14:12 *"How you are fallen from heaven,*
   O Lucifer, son of the morning!
   How you are cut down to the ground..."

In Isa 14:13-14 Lucifer said:
'I will ascend into heaven,
I will exalt my throne above the stars of God;
I will also sit on the mount of the congregation
On the farthest sides of the north;

*14 **I will** ascend above the heights of the clouds,*
***I will** be like the Most High.'* NKJV

Eight different Greek words are used to describe this organization:
    Col 11:16; Thrones, Lordships, Principalities, Authorities
    Rom 3:8; Angels, Powers
    Eph 6:12; World rulers, Spiritual powers

SERAPHIM Isa 6:1-2 *I saw the Lord sitting upon a throne, high and lifted up, and the skirts of His train filled the [most holy part of the] temple. 2 Above Him stood the seraphim; each had six wings...* AMP

CHERUBIM Ezek 1:5 *And out of the midst of it came the likeness of four living creatures [or cherubim]. And this was their appearance: they had the likeness of a man...* AMP

Ezek 10:1-2 *As I watched, I saw on the platform above the top of the cherubim something like a sapphire, resembling the shape of a throne, appearing above them. 2 The Lord said to the man dressed in linen, "Go between the wheelwork underneath the cherubim. Fill your hands with burning coals from among the cherubim and scatter them over the city." He went as I watched.* The NET Bible

Gen 3:24 *So He drove the man out; and at the east of the garden of Eden He stationed the cherubim...*

Rev 4:6 *And in front of the throne there was also what looked like a transparent glassy sea, as if of crystal. And around the throne, in the center at each side of the throne, were four living creatures (beings/cherubim)...* AMP

Large numbers of Angels in this organization
Rev 5:11 *Then I looked, and I heard the voices of many angels on every side of the throne and of the living creatures and the elders [of the heavenly Sanhedrin], and they numbered ten thousand times ten thousand and thousands of thousands...* AMP

Matt 26:53 *Do you suppose that I cannot appeal to My Father, and He will immediately provide Me with more than twelve legions [more than 80,000] of angels?* AMP

Heb 12:22 *But you have come right up into Mount Zion, to the city of the living God, the heavenly Jerusalem, and to the gathering of countless happy angels...*TLB

Deut 33:2 *He flashed forth from Mount Paran, from among ten thousands of holy ones, a flaming fire, a law, at His right hand.* AMP

2 Kings 6:17 *Then Elisha prayed, Lord, I pray You, open his eyes that he may see. And the Lord opened the young man's eyes, and he saw, and behold, the mountain was full of horses and chariots of fire round about Elisha.* AMP

Dan 7:10 ...a river of fire flowed from before him. Millions of angels ministered to him, and hundreds of millions of people stood before him, waiting to be judged. Then the court began its session, and the books were opened. TLB

ANGELS SPEAK AND RESPOND TO GOD'S WORD
Ps 103:20 *Bless the Lord, you His angels, Who excel in strength, who do His word, Heeding the voice of His word.* NKJV

1 Kings 13:18 *But the old man said, "I am a prophet too, just as you are; and an angel gave me a message from the Lord.* TLB

Heb 2:2 *For if the word spoken through angels proved unalterable...*

Luke 1:19-20 *And the angel replied to him, I am Gabriel...but my words are of a kind which will be fulfilled in the appointed and proper time.* AMP

ANGELS IN THE NEW TESTAMENT (Partial list of the Scriptures)
Luke 1:34-35 *Mary asked the angel, "But how can I have a baby? I am a virgin." 35 The angel replied, "The Holy Spirit shall come upon you...*TLB

Matt 1:20 *But as he was thinking this over, behold, an angel of the Lord appeared to him in a dream,* AMP

Luke 2:13-15 *Then suddenly there appeared with the angel an army of the troops of heaven (a heavenly knighthood), praising God and saying, 14 Glory to God in the highest [heaven], and on earth peace among men with whom He is well pleased [men of goodwill, of His favor]. 15 When the angels went away from them into heaven, the shepherds said one to another...*AMP

Matt 28:2-5 There was a violent earthquake, for an angel of the Lord came down from heaven and...5 The angel said to the women, "Do not be afraid..." NIV

Luke 22:43-44 *An angel from heaven appeared to him and strengthened him.* NIV

A BELIEVER HAS AUTHORITY OVER ANGELS

Rom 8:37-39...*we are more than conquerors and gain a surpassing victory through Him Who loved us. 38 For I am persuaded beyond doubt (am sure) that neither death nor life, nor angels nor principalities, nor things impending and threatening nor things to come, nor powers, 39 Nor height nor depth, nor anything else in all creation will be able to separate* us from the love of God which is in Christ Jesus our Lord. AMP

1 Cor 6:3 *Do you not know that we will judge angels? How much more matters of this life?*

1 Peter 3:21b-22 ...*Christ, 22 who is at the right hand of God, having gone into heaven, after angels and authorities and powers had been subjected to Him.*

Eph 2:6 And God raised us up with Christ and seated us with him in the heavenly realms in Christ Jesus...NIV

Dan 10:12 *Then he said to me, Fear not, Daniel...your words were heard, and I have come as a consequence of [and in response to] your words.* AMP

Luke 1:13 *But the angel said to him, Do not be afraid, Zachariah, because your petition was heard...*AMP

Acts 10:30-31 ...*a man stood before me in dazzling apparel, 31 And he said, Cornelius, your prayer has been heard and harkened to...* AMP

Eccl 5:6 *Do not... say before the messenger of God that it was an error.* NKJV

EVERY BELIEVER HAS AT LEAST ONE PERSONAL ANGEL

PETER'S ANGEL Acts 12:13-15 *And when he knocked at the gate of the porch, a maid named Rhoda came to answer. 14 And recognizing Peter's voice, in her joy she failed to open the gate, but ran in and told the people that Peter was standing before the porch gate. 15 They said to her, You are crazy! But she persistently and strongly and confidently affirmed that it was the truth. They said, It is his angel!* AMP

Ps 91:11-12 *For He will give His angels charge concerning you, To guard you in all your ways. 12 They will bear you up in their hands, That you do not strike your foot against a stone.*

JESUS' ANGEL, THE ANGEL OF THE LORD (or Jesus Himself)
Matt 2:13 *Now when they had gone, behold, an angel of the Lord appeared to Joseph in a dream and said, "Get up!..."*

Ex 3:2 *The angel of the Lord appeared to him in a blazing fire from the midst of a bush...*

Ex 23:23 *"For My angel will go before you and bring you in to the land..."*

Rev 1:1 *The Revelation of Jesus Christ, which God gave Him to show to His bond-servants, the things which must soon take place; and He sent and communicated it by His angel.*

Ps 34:7 *The angel of the Lord encamps around those who fear Him, And rescues them.*

GOD'S ANGEL(S) (of course, they all are His!)
Gen 31:11 *And the Angel of God said to me in the dream, Jacob. And I said, Here am I.* AMP

Gen 24:7...*He will send His Angel before you...*AMP

Dan 6:22 *My God has sent His angel and has shut the lions' mouths...*AMP

Judg 13:6 *Then the woman went and told her husband, saying, A Man of God came to me and his face was like the face of the Angel of God.* AMP

Gen 28:12 *And he dreamed that there was a ladder set up on the earth, and the top of it reached to heaven; and the angels of God were ascending and descending on it!* AMP

Ps 104:4 *He makes the winds His messengers, Flaming fire His ministers.*

YOUR ANGEL

Matt 18:10 *Beware that you do not despise or feel scornful toward or think little of one of these little ones, for I tell you that in heaven their angels always are in the presence of and look upon the face of My Father Who is in heaven.* AMP

Heb 1:14 *No, for the angels are only spirit-messengers sent out to help and care for those who are to receive his salvation.* TLB

Heb 13:2 *Do not forget or neglect or refuse to extend hospitality to strangers [in the brotherhood — being friendly, cordial, and gracious, sharing the comforts of your home and doing your part generously], for through it some have entertained angels without knowing it.* AMP

Rev 22:8-9 *And when I heard and saw, I fell down to worship at the feet of the angel who showed me these things. 9 But he said to me, "Do not do that. I am a fellow servant of yours and of your brethren the prophets and of those who heed the words of this book. Worship God."*

CHARIOTS OF GOD

Isa 66:15 *For behold, the Lord will come in fire, and His chariots will be like the stormy wind, to render His anger with fierceness, and His rebuke with flames of fire.* AMP

Ps 68:17 *The chariots of God are twenty thousand, even thousands upon thousands. The Lord is among them as He was in Sinai, [so also] in the Holy Place (the sanctuary in Jerusalem).* AMP

Hab 3:8 *You rode [before] upon Your horses and Your chariots of victory and deliverance.* AMP

2 Sam 22:11 *He rode on a cherub and flew; He was seen upon the wings of the wind.* AMP

Zech 6:1-2 *I looked up again — and there before me were four chariots coming out from between two mountains — mountains of bronze! 2 The first chariot...* NIV

Zech 1:8-10 *I saw in the night [vision] and behold, a Man riding upon a red horse, and He stood among the myrtle trees that were in a low valley or bottom, and behind Him there were horses, red, bay or flame-colored, and white. 9 Then said I, O my lord, what are these? And the angel who talked with me said, I will show you what these are. 10 And the Man who stood among the myrtle trees answered and said, These are they whom the Lord has sent to walk to and fro through the earth and patrol it.* AMP

OTHER FACTS ABOUT ANGELS FROM THE SCRIPTURES

There are Good and Bad angels. 1/3 of the angels fell with Satan and rebelled against God. Some are bound, others are loose.

Angels have:

emotions	passions	appetites
anger	desires	pride
intelligence	bodily parts	wisdom
patience	holiness	will-power
ability to speak languages		modesty
meekness		

Angels are:

glorious	immortal	powerful
mighty	sent in answer to prayer	
not to be worshipped		subject to God
organized		

Angels:

appear visible and invisible	observe us
operate in material realms	can cook
travel at inconceivable speeds	dwell in heaven
need no rest give revelations	always wear white garments
minister to saints	receive departed saints

ANOINT

Isa 61:1 *The Spirit of the Lord God is upon me, Because the Lord has anointed me To bring good news to the afflicted;*

1 John 2:20 *But you have an anointing from the Holy One*

1 John 2:27 *As for you, the anointing which you received from Him abides in you...*

James 5:14 *Is anyone among you sick? Then he must call for the elders of the church and they are to pray over him, anointing him with oil in the name of the Lord;*

John 11:2 *It was the Mary who anointed the Lord with ointment...*

Mark 6:13 *...and were anointing with oil many sick people and healing them...*

AUTHORITY OF THE BELIEVER

Prov 14:19 *The evil will bow before the good, And the wicked at the gates of the righteous.* NKJV

JESUS HAD TOTAL AUTHORITY

Matt 28:18 *Jesus approached and, breaking the silence, said to them, All authority (all power of rule) in heaven and on earth has been given to Me.* AMP

Col 2:15 *[God] disarmed the principalities and powers that were ranged against us and made a bold display and public example of them, in triumphing over them in Him and in it [the cross].* AMP

Col 2:15 *Having disarmed principalities and powers, He made a public spectacle of them, triumphing over them in it.* NKJV

John 12:31 *Now the judgment (crisis) of this world is coming on [sentence is now being passed on this world]. Now the ruler (evil genius, prince) of this world shall be cast out (expelled).* AMP

HE GAVE THAT AUTHORITY TO HIS IMMEDIATE FOLLOWERS

Luke 9:1 *THEN JESUS called together the Twelve [apostles] and gave them power and authority over all demons, and to cure diseases...*AMP

Luke 10:1 *NOW AFTER this the Lord chose and appointed seventy others and sent them out ahead of Him, two by two, into every town and place where He Himself was about to come (visit).* AMP

Luke 10:19 *Behold! I have given you authority and power to trample upon serpents and scorpions, and [physical and mental strength and ability] over all the power that the enemy [possesses]; and nothing shall in any way harm you.* AMP

DID IT WORK FOR THEM?

Acts 3:6-8 *But Peter said, "I do not possess silver and gold, but what I do have I give to you: In the name of Jesus Christ the Nazarene—walk!" 7 And seizing him by the* right hand, he raised him up; and immediately his feet and his ankles were strengthened. 8 With a leap he stood upright...

Acts 9:34 *Peter said to him, "Aeneas, Jesus Christ heals you; get up and make your bed." Immediately he got up.*

Acts 9:40 *But Peter sent them all out and knelt down and prayed, and turning to the body, he said, "Tabitha, arise." And she opened her eyes, and when she saw Peter, she sat up.*

Acts 14:10-11 (Paul)...said with a loud voice, "Stand upright on your feet." And he leaped up and began to walk.

HE GAVE AUTHORITY EVEN IN GREATER MEASURE TO THOSE WHO BELIEVE
Mark 16:17-18 *And these signs will follow those who believe: In My name they will cast out demons; they will speak with new tongues; 18 they will take up serpents; and if they drink anything deadly, it will by no means hurt them; they will lay hands on the sick, and they will recover."* NKJV

Eph 1:19-20 *...and what is the exceeding greatness of His power toward us who believe, according to the working of His mighty power 20 which He worked in Christ when He raised Him from the dead.* NKJV

Matt 16:19 *And I will give you the keys of the kingdom of heaven, and whatever you bind on earth will be bound in heaven, and whatever you loose on earth will be loosed in heaven.* NKJV

Matt 18:19-20 *"Again I say to you that if two of you agree on earth concerning anything that they ask, it will be done for them by My Father in heaven. 20 For where two or three are gathered together in My name, I am there in the midst of them."* NKJV

SUMMARY OF VERSES GIVING AUTHORITY OF ANY BELIEVER OVER SATAN
Luke 9:1 *And He called the twelve together, and gave them power and authority over all the demons and to heal diseases.*

Luke 10:19 *Behold, I have given you authority to tread on serpents and scorpions, and over all the power of the enemy, and nothing will injure you.*

Mark 16:17-18 *"...These signs will accompany those who have believed: in My name they will cast out demons, they will speak with new tongues; 18 they will pick up serpents, and if they drink any deadly poison, it will not hurt them; they will lay hands on the sick, and they will recover."*

Phil 4:13 *I can do all things through Him who strengthens me.*

Matt 28:18-19 *And Jesus came up and spoke to them, saying, "All authority has been given to Me in heaven and on earth. 19 Go therefore...*

Matt 10:1 *Jesus summoned His twelve disciples and gave them authority over unclean spirits, to cast them out, and to heal every kind of disease and every kind of sickness.*

James 4:7 *Resist the devil [stand firm against him], and he will flee from you.* AMP

Matt 4:10 *Then Jesus said to him, Begone, Satan!* AMP

Eph 4:27 *Leave no [such] room or foothold for the devil [give no opportunity to him].* AMP

Rom 16:20 *And the God of peace will soon crush Satan under your feet.* AMP

Rev 12:11 *And they have overcome (conquered) him by means of the blood of the Lamb and by the utterance of their testimony...* AMP

Luke 10:17 *The seventy returned with joy, saying, Lord, even the demons are subject to us in Your name!* AMP

Acts 16:18 *Then Paul, being sorely annoyed and worn out, turned and said to the spirit within her, I charge you in the name of Jesus Christ to come out of her! And it came out that very moment.* AMP

BAPTISM
A STUDY

TYPES OF BAPTISMS IN SCRIPTURE: (all baptisms are by burial; Rom 6:4; Col 2:12).

1. Baptism in water
Matt 3:6...*Confessing their sins, they were immersed by him in the Yarden River.* CJB

The Gk word "baptidzo" meaning "to bury into," or "to dip." Same word in Lk16:24 "dip tip of finger into water" or as "dip bread in gravy."

Acts 8:38-39 *38 He stopped the chariot, and they went down <u>into the water</u> and Philip baptized him. 39 And when they <u>came up out</u> of the water.* TLB

John 3:22 *After these things Jesus and His disciples came into the land of Judea, and there He was spending time with them and baptizing.*

Acts 10:46-47 *Then Peter answered, 47 "Surely no one can refuse the water for these to be baptized..."* (not a formula for baptism...rather, by the "authority of the Lord").

John 3:22 *After these things Jesus and His disciples came into the land of Judea, and there He was spending time with them and baptizing.*

Matt 28:19 *Go therefore and make disciples of all the nations, baptizing them in the name of the Father and the Son and the Holy Spirit.*

Acts 2:38 *"Turn from sin, return to God, and each of you be immersed on the authority of Yeshua the Messiah.* CJB

2. Baptism in suffering
Luke 12:50 *But I have a baptism to undergo, and how distressed I am until it is accomplished!*

Acts 3:18 *Thus has God fulfilled what He foretold by the mouth of all the prophets, that His Christ (the Messiah) should undergo ill treatment and be afflicted and suffer.* AMP

1 Peter 3:18 *Christ also suffered. He died once for the sins of all us guilty sinners although he himself was innocent of any sin at any time, that he might bring us safely home to God.* TLB

Matt 20:22 *But Jesus replied, You do not realize what you are asking. Are you able to drink the cup that I am about to drink and to be baptized with the baptism with which I am baptized?* AMP

Mark 10:38 *But Jesus said to them, "You do not know what you are asking. Are you able to drink the cup that I drink, or to be baptized with the baptism with which I am baptized?"*

3. Baptism into Christ

Rom 6:3-7 *Or do you not know that all of us who have been baptized into Christ Jesus have been baptized into His death? 4 Therefore we have been buried with Him through baptism into death, so that as Christ was raised from the dead... so we too....*

1 Cor 12:13 *For by one Spirit we were all baptized into one body...*

Col 2:12 *...having been buried with Him in baptism, in which you were also raised up with Him through faith in the working of God, who raised Him from the dead.*

Gal 3:27 *For all of you who were baptized into Christ have clothed yourselves with Christ.*

4. Baptism in the Holy Spirit (also see Holy Spirit)

Matt 3:11-12 *"With water I baptize those who repent of their sins; but someone else is coming, far greater than I am, so great that I am not worthy to carry his shoes! He shall baptize you with the Holy Spirit and with fire."* TLB

Acts 1:4-5 *...what the Father had promised, "Which," He said, "you heard of from Me; 5 for John baptized with water, but you will be baptized with the Holy Spirit not many days from now."*

Luke 24:49 *"And behold, I am sending forth the promise of My Father upon you; but you are to stay in the city until you are clothed with power from on high."*

THREE BAPTISMS FOR BELIEVERS

     1. Into Christ at repentance or new birth; # 3 above. Called "one baptism" because it is *the only baptism* that brings a person into the body of Christ.

     2. Water baptism after repentance; #1 above.

     3. Spirit baptism at any time after new birth; #4 above

BELIEVING FOR AN ANSWER

Matt 18:19-20 *...I say to you, that if two of you agree on earth about anything that they may ask, it shall be done for them by My Father who is in heaven. 20 For where two or three have gathered together in My name, I am there in their midst."*

Matt 19:26 *...but with God all things are possible.*

John 16:23-24 *Truly, truly, I say to you, if you ask the Father for anything in My name, He will give it to you.*

Matt 7:11 *...how much more will your Father who is in heaven give what is good to those who ask Him!*

Mark 11:24 *Therefore I say to you, all things for which you pray and ask, believe that you have received them, and they will be granted you.*

Matt 21:22 *And all things you ask in prayer, believing, you will receive.*

2 Peter 3:9 *The Lord does not delay and is not tardy or slow about what He promises...* AMP

Rom 4:16 *Therefore, [inheriting] the promise is the outcome of faith and depends [entirely] on faith...* AMP

John 14:13-14 *Whatever you ask in My name, that will I do, so that the Father may be glorified in the Son. 14 If you ask Me anything in My name, I will do it.*

Matt 7:7-8 *"Ask, and it will be given to you; seek, and you will find; knock, and it will be opened to you. 8 For everyone who asks receives, and he who seeks finds, and to him who knocks it will be opened."*

Mark 9:23-24 *And Jesus said to him, "'If You can?' All things are possible to him who believes."*

Matt 17:20 *...Jesus said to them, "Because of your unbelief; for assuredly, I say to*

you, if you have faith as a mustard seed, you will say to this mountain, 'Move from here to there,' and it will move; and nothing will be impossible for you..."
NKJV

BIND AND LOOSE

Matt 16:19 *"...whatever you bind on earth shall have been bound in heaven, and whatever you loose on earth shall have been loosed in heaven."*

Luke 11:52 *Woe to you lawyers! For you have taken away the key of knowledge; you yourselves did not enter, and you hindered those who were entering.*

Matt 23:13 *"But woe to you, scribes and Pharisees, hypocrites, because you shut off the kingdom of heaven from people; for you do not enter in yourselves, nor do you allow those who are entering to go in..."*

Matt 21:43 *"Therefore I say to you, the kingdom of God will be taken away from you and given to a people, producing the fruit of it."*

1 Kings 8:55-56 *…he stood and blessed all the assembly of Israel with a loud voice, saying: 56 "Blessed be the Lord, who has given rest to His people Israel,*

Gen 1:28 *God blessed them…*

Gen 49:28 *He blessed them, every one with the blessing appropriate to him.*

Ex 32:29 *He may bestow a blessing upon you today.*

Mal 3:10 *…open for you the windows of heaven and pour out for you a blessing until it overflows.*

Gal 3:14 *… in order that in Christ Jesus the blessing of Abraham might come to the Gentiles.*

Eph 1:3 *Blessed be the God and Father of our Lord Jesus Christ, who has blessed us with every spiritual blessing…*

1 Peter 3:8-9 *To sum up, all of you be harmonious, sympathetic, brotherly, kindhearted, and humble in spirit; 9 not returning evil for evil or insult for insult, but giving a blessing instead; for you were called for the very purpose that you might inherit a blessing.*

BLESSED WITH ABRAHAM
Gal 3:13-14 *Christ has redeemed us from the curse of the law, having become a curse for us…14 that the blessing of Abraham might come upon the Gentiles in Christ Jesus, that we might receive the promise of the Spirit through faith.* NKJV

The blessings promised to Abraham are in Deut 28:1-14
Deut 28:1-2 *IF YOU will listen diligently to the voice of the Lord your God, being watchful to do all His commandments which I command you this day, the Lord your God will set you high above all the nations of the earth. 2 And all these blessings shall come upon you and overtake you if you heed the voice of the Lord your God.* AMP

Deut 30:19-20 *"I call heaven and earth to witness against you today, that I have set before you life and death, the blessing and the curse. So choose life in order that you may live, you and your descendants, 20 by loving the Lord your God, by obeying His voice, and by holding fast to Him; for this is your life and the length of your days, that you may live in the land which the Lord swore to your fathers, to Abraham, Isaac, and Jacob, to give them."*

Because of what His Word reveals to us, you can say:
"Because I am a child of God, living by faith, I am a child of Abraham and am blessed with Abraham. The blessings to Abraham have come upon me for Galatians 3:14 says so. All the blessings of God have come upon me and have overtaken me. I say with my mouth:

"I am blessed in the City I am blessed in the
field;
My basket is blessed and so is my kneading
trough (these are my savings and checking);
I am blessed when I come in
I am blessed when I go out;
All enemies who rise up against me are defeated; they flee seven ways before me; My storehouse is blessed, the Lord has commanded it He is blessing me in the land He gives to me;
I have a surplus of prosperity in material goods;
All the work of my hands is blessed;
I lend to nations and do not borrow;
I am the head and not the tail;
I am above only and not beneath;
I do all He tells me to do;
I go not to the left nor right."

BOLDNESS

ALWAYS KNOW GOD SAYS HIS CHILDREN ARE BOLD

Jesus was bold:

John 7:26 And here He is speaking openly, and they say nothing to Him! AMP

Paul was bold:

Acts 9:29 AMP *Preaching freely and confidently and boldly in the name of the Lord*; 1 Thess 2:2...*after we had already suffered and been mistreated in Philippi, as you know, we had the boldness in our God to speak to you the gospel of God amid much opposition;* Eph 6:19 NKJV ...*that I may open my mouth boldly to make known the mystery of the gospel*

You are bold:

Prov 28:1... *the righteous are bold as a lion.*

Acts 1:8 *you will receive power when the Holy Spirit has come upon you; and you shall be My witnesses both in Jerusalem, and in all Judea and Samaria, and even to the remotest part of the earth.*

Heb 13:6 ...*we may boldly say: "The Lord is my helper; I will not fear. What can man do to me?"* NKJV

Prov 28:1 *The wicked flee when no one pursues, But the righteous are bold as a lion.* NKJV

BOLDNESS IS A QUALITY OF LIFE THAT HAS TO BE DEVELOPED

Acts 13:46 *Then Paul and Barnabas answered them boldly: "We had to speak the word of God to you first..."* NIV

Phil 1:14 ...*most of the brethren, trusting in the Lord because of my imprisonment, have far more courage to speak the word of God without fear.*

BOLDNESS DEVELOPS AS WE PRAY FOR ONE ANOTHER

41

Eph 6:19-20 *...and pray on my behalf, that utterance may be given to me in the opening of my mouth, to make known with boldness the mystery of the gospel, 20 for which I am an ambassador in chains; that in proclaiming it I may speak boldly, as I ought to speak.*

BOLDNESS DEVELOPS AS WE SPEND TIME WITH JESUS
Acts 4:13 *Now as they observed the confidence of Peter and John and understood that they were uneducated and untrained men, they were amazed, and began to recognize them as having been with Jesus.*

Eph 3:11b-12 *...in Christ Jesus our Lord, 12 in whom we have boldness and confident access through faith in Him.*

WE HAVE BOLDNESS TO COME TO THE THRONE
Heb 4:16 *Therefore let us draw near with confidence to the throne of grace, so that we may receive mercy and find grace to help in time of need.*

Heb 10:19 *Therefore, brethren, since we have confidence to enter the holy place...v 23 Let us hold fast the confession of our hope without wavering...*

OTHERS WHO WERE BOLD:

Moses: Ex 32:20	Three Hebrews: Dan 3
Elijah: 1 Kings 18:15-18	Stephen: Acts 7:51-6
Nehemiah: Neh 6:11	

CHRIST IS FORMED IN YOU TODAY

Gal 4:19 *My children, with whom I am again in labor until Christ is formed in you*

Rom 8:29 *For those whom He foreknew, He also predestined to become conformed to the image of His Son...*

Eph 4:13-14 *...until we all attain to the unity of the faith, and of the knowledge of the Son of God, to a mature man, to the measure of the stature which belongs to the fullness of Christ.*

2 Cor 5:21 *He made Him who knew no sin to be sin on our behalf, so that we might become the righteousness of God in Him.*

2 Cor 3:18 *But we all, with unveiled face, beholding as in a mirror the glory of the Lord, are being transformed into the same image from glory to glory, just as from the Lord, the Spirit.*

Eph 5:1 *THEREFORE BE imitators of God [copy Him and follow His example], as well-beloved children [imitate their father].* AMP

Eph 5:2 *And walk in love, [esteeming and delighting in one another] as Christ loved us...* AMP (we are to imitate Jesus. Walk in His steps. Walk in His love).

1 Peter 2:21 *For Christ also suffered for you, leaving you [His personal] example, so that you should follow in His footsteps.* AMP

Col 2:7 *Have the roots [of your being] firmly and deeply planted [in Him, fixed and founded in Him]...* AMP

Prov 4:18 *But the path of the righteous is like the light of dawn, that shines brighter and brighter until the full day.*

Isa 42:16 *And I will bring the blind by a way that they know not; I will lead them in paths that they have not known. I will make darkness into light before them and make uneven places into a plain.* AMP

Luke 11:36 *If then your entire body is illuminated, having no part dark, it will be wholly bright [with light], as when a lamp with its bright rays gives you light.* AMP

CONFORMED TO HIS IMAGE BY HIS WORD
Eph 4:15 *...speaking the truth in love, we are to grow up in all aspects into Him who is the head, even Christ...*

2 Peter 1:4 *He has granted to us His precious and magnificent promises, so that by them you may become partakers of the divine nature...*

John 14:21-22 *He who has My commandments and keeps them is the one who loves Me; and he who loves Me will be loved by My Father, and I will love him and will disclose Myself to him.*

1 John 2:5b-6 *...we are in Him: 6 the one who says he abides in Him ought himself to walk in the same manner as He walked.*

Eph 5:26-27 *...having cleansed her by the washing of water with the word, 27 that He might present to Himself the church in all her glory, having no spot or wrinkle or any such thing; but that she would be holy and blameless.*

John 15:10 *If you keep My commandments, you will abide in My love;*

CHRIST IS FORMED IN YOU AS YOU WALK IN LOVE
1 John 3:17 *But whoever has the world's possessions and sees his fellow Christian in need and shuts off his compassion against him, how can the love of God reside in such a person?* NET

1 John 4:16 *And we have known and believed the love that God has for us. God is love, and he who abides in love abides in God, and God in him.* NKJV

1 John 4:12 *If we love one another, God abides in us...* NKJV

Eph 5:2 *...and walk in love, just as Christ also loved you and gave Himself up for us...*

Gal 5:6 *...faith working through love.*

CHRIST IS FORMED IN YOU BY THE HOLY GHOST

Matt 3:11 *He will baptize you with the Holy Spirit and fire…*

John 14:26-27 *But the Helper, the Holy Spirit, whom the Father will send in My name, He will teach you all things, and bring to your remembrance all that I said to you.*

John 16:13 *But when He, the Spirit of truth, comes, He will guide you into all the truth;*

Titus 3:5 *He saved us, not on the basis of deeds which we have done in righteousness, but according to His mercy, by the washing of regeneration and renewing by the Holy Spirit…*

Acts 1:8 *…you will receive power when the Holy Spirit has come upon you;*

Jude 20 *…building yourselves up on your most holy faith, praying in the Holy Spirit…*

1 Cor 14:4 *One who speaks in a tongue edifies himself…*

Mt 3: 11-12 *He shall baptize you with the Holy Ghost, and with fire…*

COMPASSION

Compassion is <u>not</u> pity, feeling sorry for someone, not helping the situation. It <u>moves in</u> on the situation and brings the Word of deliverance.

Mark 1:40-41 *And a leper came to Jesus, beseeching Him and falling on his knees before Him, and saying, "If You are willing, You can make me clean." 41 Moved with compassion, Jesus stretched out His hand and touched him, and said to him, "I am willing; be cleansed."* KJV

Ps 86:15 *But You, O Lord, are a God full of compassion, and gracious, Longsuffering and abundant in mercy and truth.* NKJV

Heb 4:15 *For we do not have a High Priest Who is unable to understand and sympathize and have a shared feeling with our weaknesses.* AMP

Matt 8:17 *He Himself took [in order to carry away] our weaknesses and infirmities* and *bore away our diseases.* AMP   skh

James 5:11 *...the Lord is full of compassion and is merciful.*

2 Kings 13:23 *But the Lord was gracious to them and had compassion on them and turned to them because of His covenant with Abraham.*

Mic 7:19 *He will again have compassion on us; He will tread our iniquities under foot.*

Matt 9:36-37 *Seeing the people, He felt compassion for them, because they were distressed and dispirited like sheep without a shepherd.*

Mark 8:2 *I feel compassion for the people...*

2 Cor 1:3-4 *God of all comfort, 4 who comforts us in all our affliction so that we will be able to comfort those who are in any affliction with the comfort with which we ourselves are comforted by God.*

Matt 14:14 *And when Jesus went out He saw a great multitude; and He was moved with compassion for them...* NKJV

Rom 9:15 *For He says to Moses, "I will have mercy on whomever I will have mercy, and I will have compassion on whomever I will have compassion...* NKJV

CONTENTMENT

Lev 10:20 *And when Moses heard that, he was content.* KJV

1 Tim 6:8 *And having food and raiment let us be therewith content.* KJV

Phil 4:11 *Not that I speak in respect of want: for I have learned, in whatsoever state I am, therewith to be content.* KJV

During the eighteenth century, an English clergyman wrote five rules to remain contented:
1. Allow yourself to complain of nothing, not even of the weather.

2. Do not imagine yourself to be somewhere other than where you are.

3. Do not compare your situation with that of anyone else.

4. Never allow yourself to dwell on wishing this or that had happened. Remember, God Almighty lovers you better and more wisely than you love yourself.

5. Never dwell on tomorrow. Remind yourself that tomorrow is in God's hands, not yours. The heaviest part of sorrow is often looking forward to it with dread. Remember, the Lord will provide.

CROWNS

REWARD OF CROWNS

1. Incorruptible Crown

1 Cor 9:25-26 *Everyone who competes in the games goes into strict training. They do it to get a crown that will not last; but we do it to get a crown that will last forever.* NIV

2. Crown of Righteousness

2 Tim 4:7-8 *Finally, there is laid up for me the crown of righteousness, which the Lord, the righteous Judge, will give to me on that Day, and not to me only but also to all who have loved His appearing.* NKJV

3. Crown of Life

James 1:12-13 *Blessed is a man who perseveres under trial; for once he has been approved, he will receive the crown of life which the Lord has promised to those who love Him.*

Rev 2:10-11 *Be faithful until death, and I will give you the crown of life.*

4. Crown of Glory

1 Peter 5:4 *And when the Chief Shepherd appears, you will receive the unfading crown of glory.*

To be Guarded

Rev 3:11 *I am coming quickly; hold fast what you have, so that no one will take your crown.*

Cast at Jesus' Feet

Rev 4:10 *...cast their crowns before the throne...*

Symbolic Crowns

1. Crown of Soul Winner

Phil 4:1 *THEREFORE, MY brethren, whom love and yearn to see, my delight and crown (wreath of victory), thus stand firm in the Lord, my beloved.* AMP

1 Thess 2:19 *For who is our hope or joy or crown of exultation? Is it not even you...*

2. Crown of Honor

Job 19:9 *"He has stripped my honor from me And removed the crown from my head.*

Pro 12:4 *"A virtuous woman is a crown to her husband ..."* KJV

Pro 17:6 *"Children's children (grandchildren) are the crown of old men ... "* KJV

Pro 4:9 *" .... a crown of glory shall she (God's Wisdom) deliver to thee."* KJV

Isa 28:1-5 *"Woe to the crown of pride .... trodden Under feet."* KJV

DEATH
A STUDY

At the time of death, only the *physical body* goes into the grave, waiting to be changed and resurrected at either the rapture (the believer's body) or the Great White Throne Judgment (the un believer's body). The *spirit and soul* immediately are taken either to heaven (paradise) or to Hell (Hades). The spirit, soul, and body of every person will be re-united at a resurrection (either the rapture or the Great White Throne Judgment). Death in the Bible is separation or a cutting off. Physical death is a separation of the soul and spirit from the body.

75 times the Bible says the physical body goes to the grave (*qeber*, a place at the earth). It also says life on earth is short lived and compares it to:

1. **A pilgrimage**; Gen 47:9 *And Jacob said to Pharaoh, "The days of the years of my pilgrimage are one hundred and thirty years; few and evil have been the days of the years of my life, and they have not attained to the days of the years of the life of my fathers in the days of their pilgrimage."* NKJV

2. **A dream**; Ps 73:20 *Their present life is only a dream!* TLB

3. **Water spilled on the ground**; *2 Sam 14:14 All of us must die eventually; our lives are like water that is poured out on the ground.* TLB

4. **Wind**; Job 7:7 *Oh, remember that my life is a breath!* NKJV

5. **Sleep that is soon over**; Ps 90:5 *You carry away [these disobedient people, doomed to die within forty years] as with a flood; they are as a sleep [vague and forgotten as soon as they are gone].* AMP

6. **A passing cloud**; Job 7:9 *As the cloud disappears and vanishes away, So he who goes down to the grave does not come up.* NKJV

7. **A shadow**; Ps 144:4 *Man is like a breath; His days are like a passing shadow.* NKJV Job 14:2 *He flees like a shadow and does not continue.* NKJV

8. **Flowers that fade away**; Job 14:2 He blossoms for a moment like a flower-and withers. TLB Ps 103:15-16 *...our days are few and brief, like grass, like flowers, 16 blown by the wind and gone forever.* TLB

9. **Grass that dies**; Ps 103:15-16 ... our days are few and brief, like grass...16 blown by the wind and gone forever. TLB

10. **Green herbs that wither**; Ps 37:2b *...fade like the green herb*

THREE TYPES OF DEATH

1. Physical death; separation of the inner man from the outer man. James 2:26 *...the body without the spirit is dead...*

2. Spiritual death; separation of man from God because of sin. 1 Tim 5:6 *But she who gives herself to wanton pleasure is dead even while she lives.*

   Eph 2:1 *And you were dead in your trespasses and sins...*

   Isa 59:2 *But your iniquities have made a separation between you and your God, And your sins have hidden His face from you so that He does not hear.*

   Col 2:13 *When you were dead in your transgressions...*

3. Eternal death; Eternal separation from God in the lake of fire. Matt 10:28 *And do not be afraid of those who kill the body but cannot kill the soul; but rather be afraid of Him who can destroy both soul and body in hell (Gehenna).* AMP

   Rev 2:11 *He who overcomes (is victorious) shall in no way be injured by the second death.* AMP

   Rev 14:9-10 *Anyone worshiping the Creature from the sea and his statue, and accepting his mark on the forehead or the hand 10 must drink the wine of the anger of God; it is poured out undiluted into God's* cup of wrath. And they will be tormented with fire and burning Sulphur. TLB

Luke 16:22-23 *And it occurred that the man [reduced to] begging died and was carried by the angels to Abraham's bosom. The rich man also died and was buried. 23 And in Hades (the realm of the dead), being in torment...* AMP

Rev 20:13-15 *...and they were judged, every one of them according to their deeds. 14 Then death and Hades were thrown into the lake of fire. This is the second death, the lake of fire. 15 And if anyone's name was not found written in the book of life, he was thrown into the lake of fire.*

Isa 66:24 *"Then they will go forth and look On the corpses of the men Who have transgressed against Me. For their worm will not die And their fire will not be quenched; And they will be an abhorrence to all mankind."*

DEATH IS FACTUAL

Gen 3:19 *By the sweat of your face You will eat bread,*
Till you return to the ground,
Because from it you were taken;
For you are dust,
And to dust you shall return."

- Rom 5:12 *Therefore, just as through one man sin entered the world, and death through sin, and thus death spread to all men, because all sinned.* NKJV

- 1 Cor 15:21 *For since death came through a man (Adam)...*CJB

- Heb 9:27 *And inasmuch as it is appointed for men to die once and after this comes judgment...*

Heb 2:14-15 *Therefore, since the children share in flesh and blood, He Himself likewise also partook of the same, that through death He might render powerless him who had the power of death, that is, the devil, 15 and might free those who through fear of death were subject to slavery all their lives.*

Mark 12:25 *For when they rise from the dead...* (speaking of the body)

- 2 Cor 5:6-8 *...we are at home in the body we are absent from the Lord— 7 for we walk by faith, not by sight— 8 we are of good courage, I say, and prefer rather to be absent from the body and to be at home with the Lord.*

- Phil 1:21 *For to me, to live is Christ and to die is gain.*

- Phil 1:23-24 *But I am hard-pressed from both directions, having the desire to depart and be with Christ, for that is very much better; 24 yet to remain on in the flesh is more necessary for your sake.*

- 2 Peter 1:14 *I know that I'm to die soon; the Master has made that quite clear to me.* MS

SLEEP REFERRING TO DEATH

John 11:11-13 *This He said, and after that He said to them, "Our friend Lazarus has fallen asleep; but I go, so that I may awaken him out of sleep." 12 The disciples then said to Him, "Lord, if he has fallen asleep, he will recover." 13 Now Jesus has spoken of his death, but they thought that He was speaking of literal sleep.*

1 Thess 4:13a-16 *But we do not want you to be uninformed, brethren, about those who are asleep...14b even so God will bring with Him those who have fallen asleep in Jesus. 15b...we who are alive and remain until the coming of the Lord, will not precede those who have fallen asleep. 16b...and the dead in Christ will rise first.*

1 Thess 5:10-11 *...that whether we are awake or asleep, we will live together with Him.*

Acts 7:60 *Then falling on his knees, he cried out with a loud voice, "Lord, do not hold this sin against them!" Having said this, he fell asleep.*

1 Cor 11:30 For this reason many among you are weak and sick, and a number sleep.

1 Cor 15:17-18 ...if Christ has not been raised, your faith is worthless; you are still in your sins. 18 Then those also who have fallen asleep in Christ have perished.

EXPLANATION OF "GHOST" IN THE KJV

Used 11 times in the O.T. and 8 times in the N.T. The meaning is to "breath out, expire and die. It means "guest." Examples:

Gen 25:8 *Then Abraham gave up the ghost, and died in a good old age* KJV

Gen 25:8 *Then Abraham's spirit was released, and he died at a good (ample, full) old age, an old man, satisfied.* AMP

Gen 35:29 *And Isaac gave up the ghost, and died* KJV

Gen 35:29 *And Isaac's spirit departed; he died* AMP

Acts 5:10 *Then fell she down straightway at his feet, and yielded up the ghost: and the young men came in, and found her dead.* KJV

Acts 5:10 *And instantly she fell down at his feet and died; and the young men entering found her dead.* AMP

Acts 5:5 *And Ananias hearing these words fell down, and gave up the ghost:* KJV

Acts 5:5 *Upon hearing these words, Ananias fell down and died.* AMP

Ps 116:15 *Precious (important and no light matter) in the sight of the Lord is the death of His saints (His loving ones).* AMP

DEBT OR BORROWING (also see Interest)

God has never manifested Himself through a loan. He does not prohibit using credit. He simply sets down principles on how it should be used. (1) It should not be long term. (2) It should never be normal for God's people. (3) Never take on an obligation without a certain method and plan for repayment.

Prov 22:7 *The rich rules over the poor, And the borrower becomes the lender's slave.*

Deut 28:12 *...you shall lend to many nations.*

Rom 13:8 *Keep out of debt and owe no man anything, except to love one another.* AMP

Deut 15:6 *When the Lord your God blesses you as He promised you, then you shall lend to many nations, but you shall not borrow; and you shall rule over many nations, but they shall not rule over you.* AMP

Matt 5:42 *Give to him who keeps on begging from you, and do not turn away from him who would borrow [at interest] from you.* AMP

Ps 112:5 *It is well with the man who deals generously and lends, who conducts his affairs with justice.* AMP

Ps 37:21 *The wicked borrow and pay not again [for they may be unable], but the [uncompromisingly] righteous deal kindly and give [for they are able].* AMP

Ex 22:14 *If a man borrows anything from his neighbor, and it is injured or dies while its owner is not with it, he shall make full restitution.*

DECISION-DECREE-DECLARE

Job 22:28 *You shall also decide and decree a thing, and it shall be established for you...* AMP

MAKE A FIRM DECISION according to what is right in His sight, found in His Word.
Deut 30:19 *I have set before you life and death, the blessings and the curses; therefore choose life...* AMP

MAKE THE DECREE IN HIS NAME. Announce it as in effect from out of your spirit.
Col 3:17 *...do all in the name of the Lord Jesus...*

Mark 11:22-24 Have faith in God. 23 "Truly I say to you, whoever says to this mountain, 'Be taken up and cast into the sea,' and does not doubt in his heart, but believes that what he says is going to happen, it will be granted him."

John 1:12-13 *...those who believe in His name...*

Acts 3:16 *And on the basis of faith in His name...*

DECLARE IT FORTH WITH YOUR MOUNTH AND ACTIONS. Walk and talk as if it is so, thanking Him that He performs His Word.
Ps 119:13-16 *13 I proclaim with my mouth all the rulings you have spoken. 14 I rejoice in the way of your instruction more than in any kind of wealth. 15 I will meditate on your precepts and keep my eyes on your ways. 16 I will find my delight in your regulations.* I will not forget your word. CJB

Matt 16:19b *Whatever you prohibit on earth will be prohibited in heaven, and whatever you permit on earth will be permitted in heaven.* CJB

Ps 2:7a *I will declare the decree: The Lord has said to Me...* NKJV

2 Cor 4:18 *While we look not at the things which are seen, but at the things which are not seen...* KJV

DELIVERANCE

A STUDY

Deliverance, to set free; restore; rescue. There are 25 Hebrew words translated "deliver." Most of them deal with an enemy and sickness. You may have an enemy come against you and attempt to steal, kill, or destroy what you have. That enemy may (or may not) be the originator of your physical problem.

Ps 44:4 You are my King, O God; command victories and deliverance for Jacob (Israel). AMP

Ps 68:20 God is to us a God of deliverances... AMP

DELIVERED BY GOD'S STRENGTH AND NOT MAN'S

Ps 33:17-19 *A horse is a vain hope for safety; Neither shall it deliver any by its great strength. 18 Behold, the eye of the Lord is on those who fear Him, On those who hope in His mercy, 19 To deliver their soul from death, And to keep them alive in famine.* NKJV

Isa 50:2 *Is My hand so short that it cannot ransom? Or have I no power to deliver? Behold, I dry up the sea with My rebuke...*

Jer 1:8 *"Do not be afraid of them, For I am with you to deliver you,"* declares the Lord.

2 Sam 22:20 *He also brought me out into a broad place; He delivered me because He delighted in me.* NKJV

Ex 15:6 *Your right hand, O Lord, has become glorious in power; Your right hand, O Lord, has dashed the enemy in pieces.* NKJV

Ps 32:7 *You are my hiding place; You shall preserve me from trouble; You shall surround me with songs of deliverance.* NKJV

DELIVERED BY ANGELS

Ps 34:7 *The angel of the Lord encamps all around those who fear Him, And delivers them.* NKJV

2 Kings 6:17 *And Elisha prayed, and said, "Lord, I pray, open his eyes that he may see." Then the Lord opened the eyes of the young man, and he saw. And behold, the mountain was full of horses and chariots of fire all around Elisha.* NKJV

Ps 91:11-12 *For He shall give His angels charge over you, To keep you in all your ways. 12 In their hands they shall bear you up, Lest you dash your foot against a stone.* NKJV

Dan 6:22 *My God sent His angel and shut the lions' mouths, so that they have not hurt me...* NKJV

DELIVERED THROUGH JESUS CHRIST
Rom 8:32 *He who did not spare His own Son, but delivered Him over for us all, how will He not also with Him freely give us all things?*

Gal 1:3-5 *...our Lord Jesus Christ, 4 who gave Himself for our sins, that He might deliver us from this present evil age, according to the will of our God and Father, 5 to whom be glory forever and ever. Amen.* NKJV

Luke 4:18 *The Spirit of the Lord [is] upon Me, because He has anointed Me [the Anointed One, the Messiah] to preach the good news (the Gospel) to the poor; He has sent Me to announce release to the captives and recovery of sight to the blind, to send forth as delivered those who are oppressed [who are downtrodden, bruised,* crushed, and broken down by calamity]... AMP

Joel 2:32 *And it will come about that whoever calls on the name of the Lord Will be delivered...*

Matt 6:13 *And do not lead us into temptation, but deliver us from evil.*

DELIVERANCE COMES THROUGH THE WORD
Ps 107:20 *He sent His word and healed them, And delivered them from their destructions.*

John 8:31-32 *If you continue in My word, then you are truly disciples of Mine; 32 and you will know the truth...*

Matt 8:16 *And He cast out the spirits with a word.* NKJV

Ps 17:4 *By the word of Your lips, I have kept away from the paths of the destroyer.* NKJV

Ps 119:153 *Consider my affliction and deliver me, For I do not forget Your law.* NKJV

DELIVERANCE COMES WHEN WE BELIEVE
Ps 32:7 *You are my hiding place; You preserve me from trouble; You surround me with songs of deliverance.*

1 Chron 11:14 *...they made a stand in the middle of that area. They defended it... the Lord gave them a great victory.* The NET Bible

Ps 34:4 *I sought the Lord's help and he answered me; he delivered me from all my fears.* NET

Ps 18:2 *The Lord is my rock and my fortress and my deliverer, My God, my rock, in whom I take refuge...*

DELIVERED FROM PHYSICAL VIOLENCE
Dan 3:17 *...he will save us from the blazing hot furnace and from your power.* CJB

2 Tim 4:17 *I was rescued from the lion's mouth.* CJB

Ps 144:10 *...you save your servant David from the cruel sword.* CJB

KNOW THAT GOD DELIVERS *'OUT OF'* NOT *'INTO'*
See Pro 11:8, Ps 144:7, 107:6, 91:3, 34:19, and Job 36:15

DELIVERED ...
"from lion and bear" (1 Sam 17:35-37}
"from my strong enemy" (Ps 18:17)
"from the violent man" (Ps 18:38)
"from all my fears (Ps 34:4)
"out of trouble" (Ps 54:7)
"of all afflictions" (Acts 7:10)
"from power of darkness" (Col 1:13)

Diligence means perseverance, zeal, or, as it is used in most of these scriptures in the Hebrew, determination. So, insert the idea of perseverance, zeal, and determination in each of these scriptures in place of the word diligent.

THE DILIGENT MAN SHALL STAND BEFORE IMPORTANT MEN
Prov 22:29 *Do you see a man who excels in his work? He will stand before kings; He will not stand before unknown men.* NKJV

THE DILIGENT MAN BECOMES RICH IN GOD
Prov 10:4-5 *He who has a slack hand becomes poor, But the hand of the diligent makes rich. 5 He who gathers in summer is a wise son; He who sleeps in harvest is a son who causes shame.* NKJV

Prov 12:11 *He who tills his land will have plenty of bread, But he who pursues worthless things lacks sense.*

THE DILIGENT MAN RULES OVER CIRCUMSTANCES
Prov 12:24 *The hand of the diligent will rule, But the slack hand will be put to forced labor.*

Ps 110:2 *"Rule in the midst of Your enemies."*

2 Peter 1:3 *His divine power has granted to us everything pertaining to life and godliness, through the true knowledge of Him who called us by His own glory and excellence.*

Isa 14:2 *...they will rule over their [former] oppressors.* AMP

THE DILIGENT MAN'S THOUGHTS BRING HIM VICTORY
Prov 21:5 *The thoughts of the [steadily] diligent tend only to plenteousness...* AMP

Prov 23:7 *For as he thinks in his heart, so is he.* AMP

Prov 13:4 *Lazy people want much but get little, while the diligent are prospering.* TLB

THE DILIGENT MAN IS STEADFAST IN GOD

1 Cor 15:58 *Therefore, my beloved brethren, be steadfast, immovable, always abounding in the work of the Lord, knowing that your toil is not in vain in the Lord.*

Eph 6:10 *...be strong in the Lord and in the strength of His might.*

*D*ISCIPLINE

Col 3:22-24 *Servants, obey in everything those who are your earthly masters, not only when their eyes are on you as pleasers of men, but in simplicity of purpose [with all your heart] because of your reverence for the Lord and as a sincere expression of your devotion to Him. 23 Whatever may be your task, work at it heartily (from the soul), as [something done] for the Lord and not for men, 24 Knowing [with all certainty] that it is from the Lord [and not from men] that you will receive the inheritance which is your [real] reward. [The One Whom] you are actually serving [is] the Lord Christ (the Messiah).* AMP

Heb 12:1 *THEREFORE THEN, since we are surrounded by so great a cloud of witnesses [who have borne testimony to the Truth], let us strip off and throw aside every encumbrance (unnecessary weight) and that sin which so readily (deftly and cleverly) clings to and entangles us, and let us run with patient endurance and steady and active persistence the appointed course of the race that is set before us...v. 11 For the time being no discipline brings joy, but seems grievous and painful; but afterwards it yields a peaceable fruit of righteousness to those who have been trained by it...* AMP   skh

DISCOURAGEMENT

Behind every discouragement is a lie from Satan.

Heb 6:18 *This was so that, by two unchangeable things [His promise and His oath] in which it is impossible for God ever to prove false or deceive us, we who have fled [to Him] for refuge might have mighty indwelling strength and strong encouragement to grasp and hold fast the hope appointed for us and set before [us].* AMP

Prov 12:25 *Anxiety in a man's heart weighs it down, but an encouraging word makes it glad.* AMP

Prov 15:13 *A glad heart makes a cheerful countenance, but by sorrow of heart the spirit is broken.* AMP

Prov 15:15 *All the days of the desponding* (discouraged, by author) *and afflicted are made evil [by anxious thoughts and forebodings], but he who has a glad heart has a continual feast [regardless of circumstances].* AMP

Prov 23:7 *For as he thinks in his heart, so is he.* AMP. Do not allow discouraging thoughts to give birth in you.

Ps 39:13 *O look away from me and spare me, that I may recover cheerfulness and encouraging strength and know gladness before I go and am no more!* AMP

Skh

Spend more time reading His Words than feeding the physical body. Feed the physical body good food.

Ps 119:103 *How sweet are Your words to my taste, sweeter than honey to my mouth!* AMP

Ps 19:9-11 *God's laws are pure, eternal, just. 10 They are more desirable than gold. They are sweeter than honey dripping from a honeycomb.* TLB

Isa 55:2 *Why do you spend your money for that which is not bread, and your earnings for what does not satisfy? Hearken diligently to Me, and eat what is good, and let your soul delight itself in fatness [the profuseness of spiritual joy].* AMP

Rom 13:14 *...clothe yourself with the Lord Jesus Christ (the Messiah), and make no provision for [indulging] the flesh.* AMP

Ps 23:1 *The Lord is my shepherd, I shall not want.*

Ps 34:8 *O taste and see that the Lord is good;*

Phil 4:8 *For the rest, brethren, whatever is true, whatever is worthy of reverence and is honorable and seemly, whatever is just, whatever is pure, whatever is lovely and lovable, whatever is kind and winsome and gracious, if there is any virtue and excellence, if there is anything worthy of praise, think on and weigh and take account of these things [fix your minds on them].* AMP

Rom 8:13 *For if you live according to [the dictates of] the flesh, you will surely die* AMP

Gal 5:24 *Now those who belong to Christ Jesus have crucified the flesh with its passions and desires.*

Prov 23:2-3 *And put a knife to your throat If you are a man of great appetite. 3 Do not desire his delicacies, For it is deceptive food.*

FAITH

A STUDY

Faith is a concrete conviction and the active practice built on trust and belief in God.

FAITH SCRIPTURES
Rom 12:3 *For through the grace given to me I say to everyone among you not to think more highly of himself than he ought to think; but to think so as to have sound judgment, as God has allotted to each a measure of faith.*

Rom 10:16-17 *WHO HAS BELIEVED OUR REPORT?" 17 So faith comes from hearing, and hearing by the word of Christ.*

Rom 10:8 *But what does it say? "THE WORD IS NEAR YOU, IN YOUR MOUTH AND IN YOUR HEART"—that is, the word of faith which we are preaching...*

Heb 11:1 *NOW FAITH is the assurance (the confirmation, the title deed) of the things [we] hope for, being the proof of things [we] do not see and the conviction of their reality [faith perceiving as real fact what is not revealed to the senses].* AMP

Heb 12:2 *Looking away [from all that will distract] to Jesus, Who is the Leader and the Source of our faith [giving the first incentive for our belief] and is also its Finisher [bringing it to maturity and perfection].* AMP

Mark 11:22-23 *And Jesus, replying, said to them, Have faith in God [constantly]. 23 Truly I tell you, whoever says to this mountain, Be lifted up and thrown into the sea! and does not doubt at all in his heart but believes that what he says will take place, it will be done for him.* AMP

James 2:17 *Even so faith, if it has no works, is dead, being by itself.*

Gal 5:6 *For in Christ Jesus neither circumcision nor uncircumcision means anything, but faith working through love.*

Gal 3:7-14 *Know and understand that it is [really] the people [who live] by faith who are [the true] sons of Abraham. 9 So then, those who are people of faith are blessed and made happy and favored by God [as partners in fellowship] with the believing and trusting Abraham. 13 Christ purchased our freedom [redeeming us] from the curse (doom) of the Law [and its condemnation] by [Himself] becoming a curse for us, for it is written [in the Scriptures], Cursed is everyone who hangs on a tree (is crucified); [Deut 21:23.] 14 To the end that through [their receiving] Christ Jesus, the blessing [promised] to Abraham might come upon the Gentiles, so that we through faith might [all] receive [the realization of] the promise of the [Holy] Spirit.* AMP

FAITH IS A LAW OF GOD.
This law believes the Word and acts on it by doing and/or saying it.

Rom 3:27...*by the law of faith.* NKJV

Mark 11:23-24 *For assuredly, I say to you, whoever says to this mountain, 'Be removed and be cast into the sea,' and does not doubt in his heart, but believes that those things he says will be done, he will have whatever he says. 24 Therefore I say to you, whatever things you ask when you pray, believe that you receive them, and you will have them.* NKJV

2 Cor 4:13 And since we have the same spirit of faith, according to what is written, "I believed and therefore I spoke," we also believe and therefore speak... NKJV

Matt 12:34 ...*out of the abundance of the heart the mouth speaks.* NKJV

Prov 23:7 *For as he thinks in his heart, so is he.* NKJV

Rom 10:8-11 *But what does it say? "The word is near you, in your mouth and in your heart" (that is, the word of faith which we preach): 9 that if you confess with your mouth the Lord Jesus and believe in your heart that God has raised Him from the dead, you will be saved. 10 For with the heart one believes unto righteousness, and with the mouth confession is made unto salvation.* NKJV

FAITH DEVELOPS FROM THE WORD
Rom 10:17 ...*faith comes by hearing, and hearing by the word of God.* NKJV

Acts 11:13-14 *And he told us how he had seen an angel standing in his house, who said to him, 'Send men to Joppa, and call for Simon... 14 who will tell you words by which you and all your household will be saved.'* NKJV

Acts 14:7-11 *And they were preaching the gospel there. 8 And in Lystra a certain man without strength in his feet was sitting, a cripple from his mother's womb, who had never walked. 9 This man heard Paul speaking. Paul, observing him intently and seeing that he had faith to be healed, 10 said with a loud voice, "Stand up straight on your feet!" And he leaped and walked.* NKJV

Acts 8:5-8 *Then Philip went down to the city of Samaria and preached Christ to them. 6 And the multitudes with one accord heeded the things spoken by Philip, hearing and seeing the miracles which he did. 7 For unclean spirits, crying with a loud voice, came out of many who were possessed; and many who were paralyzed and lame were healed. 8 And there was great joy in that city.* NKJV

ALL BELIEVERS HAVE FAITH

Rom 12:3 *...God has allotted to each a measure of faith.* Every person begins life with the measure of God's faith, it then grows by hearing God's Word.

Rom 10:17 *...faith comes from hearing...*

2 Thess 3:2 *...unreasonable and wicked men; for not all have faith.* NKJV. Speaking about unreasonable, wicked men. Apparently, the measure of faith is lost if it never grows from hearing the Word.

WHERE IS THIS FAITH?

Rom 10:7-8 *But what does it say? "The word is near you, in your mouth and in your heart" (that is, the word of faith which we preach).* NKJV

HOW IMPORTANT IS FAITH?

Heb 10:38 *But the just shall live by faith.* AMP

1 John 5:4 *And this is the victory that has overcome the world — our faith.* NKJV

Heb 11:6 *And without faith it is impossible to please Him...*

Rom 14:23 *...whatever is not from faith is sin.* NKJV

Eph 2:8 *For by grace you have been saved through faith...*NKJV

Rom 5:1 *...having been justified by faith, we have peace with God.* NKJV

Acts 26:18 *...sanctified by faith in Me.* NKJV

Matt 9:29 *"According to your faith let it be to you."* NKJV

James 5:15 *And the prayer of faith will save the sick.* NKJV

Eph 6:16 *...taking the shield of faith with which you will be able to quench all the fiery darts of the wicked one.* NKJV

1 John 5:4 *And this is the victory that has overcome the world — our faith.* NKJV

THERE ARE LEVELS OF FAITH

Mark 4:40 *Do you still have **no** faith?*

Matt 16:8 *You men of **little** faith...*

Rom 4:19 *...becoming **weak** in faith*

Rom 4:20 *...he did not waver in unbelief but grew **strong** in faith...*

Acts 6:5 *...a man **full** of faith*

Matt 15:28 *...your faith is **great**;*

Matt 8:10 *I have not found **such great faith** with anyone in Israel.*

Matt 9:22 ***your faith** has made you well.*

1 Cor 13:2 *...if I have **all** faith...*

Rom 1:17 *...from **faith to faith**;*

Col 2:7 *...having been **firmly rooted** and now **being built up** in Him and **established** in your faith...*

Luke 17:5-6 *"Increase our faith!"*

FAMILY/HOME

THE HOME

- Gen 2:7 *Then the Lord God formed man of dust from the ground, and breathed into his nostrils...*

- Gen 2:18, 21, 22 *Now the Lord God said, It is not good (sufficient, satisfactory) that the man should be alone; I will make him a helper meet (suitable, adapted, complementary) for him. 21 And the Lord God caused a deep sleep to fall upon Adam; and while he slept, He took one of his ribs or a part of his side and closed up the [place with] flesh. 22 And the rib or part of his side which the Lord God had taken from the man He built up and made into a woman, and He brought her to the man. AMP*

God did away with the law of addition. In this instance, one was added to one and together became one...The first family.

Prov 3:33 *He declares blessed (joyful and favored with blessings) the home of the just and consistently righteous. AMP*

Heb 13:4 *Let marriage be held in honor (esteemed worthy, precious, of great price, and especially dear) in all things. And thus let the marriage bed be undefiled... AMP*

Gen 2:24 *Therefore a man shall leave his father and his mother and shall become united and cleave to his wife, and they shall become one flesh. AMP*

1 Tim 3:4-5 *He must rule his own household well, keeping his children under control, with true dignity, commanding their respect in every way and keeping them respectful. 5 For if a man does not know how to rule his own household, how is he to take care of the church of God? AMP*

Mark 10:9
What therefore God has united (joined together), let not man separate or divide. AMP

Gen 1:26 *God said, Let Us [Father, Son, and Holy Spirit] make mankind in Our image, after Our likeness, and let them have complete authority over* (everything). AMP

SEE 1 Cor 7

THE HUSBAND

Gen 2:7 *...the Lord God formed man from the dust of the ground and breathed into his nostrils the breath or spirit of life, and man became a living being.* AMP

Prov 31:11 *The heart of her husband trusts in her confidently and relies on and believes in her securely, so that he has no lack of [honest] gain or need of [dishonest] spoil.* AMP

1 Cor 7:2 *...let each [man] have his own wife.* AMP. Any man may take a wife, but not mandatory for all men.

Eph 5:23 *For the husband is head of the wife as Christ is the Head of the church.* AMP

Col 3:19 *Husbands, love your wives [be affectionate and sympathetic with them] and do not be harsh or bitter or resentful toward them.* AMP

1 Tim 3:2-4 *An overseer, then, must be above reproach, the husband of one wife, temperate, prudent, respectable, hospitable, able to teach, 3 not addicted to wine or pugnacious, but gentle, peaceable, free from the love of money. 4 He must be one who manages his own household well, keeping his children under control with all dignity*

1 Peter 3:7 *You husbands in the same way, live with your wives in an understanding way, as with someone weaker* (MORE DELECATE, added by author), *since she is a woman; and show her honor as a fellow heir of the grace of life, so that your prayers will not be hindered.*

Eph 5:28 *...husbands ought also to love their own wives as their own bodies. He who loves his own wife loves himself...*

71

Eph 5:33 *Nevertheless, each individual among you also is to love his own wife even as himself.*

Eph 6:4 *And now a word to you parents. Don't keep on scolding and nagging your children, making them angry and resentful. Rather, bring them up with the loving discipline the Lord himself approves, with suggestions and godly advice.* TLB

EIGHT COMMANDS FOR HUSBANDS FROM EPHESIANS 5
1. Be head of the wife like Christ heads His Church...v. 23
2. Love your wife as Christ loves the Church...v. 25
3. Love your wife as your own body...vs. 28, 33
4. Care for her, protect her...v. 29
5. Cherish her...v. 29; 1 Tim 2:7
6. Be joined with her as one flesh...v. 30-31
7. Leave your parents, begin a new family...v. 31
8. Be joined to your wife...v. 31; Matt 19:5

THE WIFE

"Woman" in Hebrew, meant she-man, womb-man or man-with-the-womb. Woman is said not to have been taken out of man's head to be lorded over by him, nor from his feet to be trampled on by him, but from his side to be equal with him, from under arm to be protected by him and from near his heart to be loved by him.

Gen 2:18, 21-22 *Then the Lord God said, "It is not good for the man to be alone; I will make him a helper suitable for him." Vs. 21-22... then He took one of his ribs and closed up the flesh at that place. 22 The Lord God fashioned* (BUILDED, SKILLFULLY FORMED; not the ordinary Hebrew word for "made." Added by author) *into a woman the rib which He had taken from the man and brought her to the man.*

Prov 19:14 *...only the Lord can give them understanding wives.* TLB

Prov 18:22 *He who finds a wife finds a good thing And obtains favor from the Lord.*

Prov 21:9 *It is better to live in a corner of a roof Than in a house shared with a contentious woman.*

1 Cor 7:2 *...each woman is to have her own husband.*
1 Tim 3:11-12 *Their wives must be thoughtful, not heavy drinkers, not gossipers, but faithful in everything they do. 12 Deacons should have only one wife, and they should have happy, obedient families.* TLB

Titus 2:4-5 *So that they will wisely train the young women to be sane and sober of mind (temperate, disciplined) and to love their husbands and their children...5 To be self-controlled, chaste, homemakers, good-natured (kindhearted), adapting and subordinating themselves to their husbands, that the word of God may not be exposed to reproach (blasphemed or discredited).* AMP

1 Peter 3:1-2 *IN LIKE manner, you married women, be submissive to your own husbands [subordinate yourselves as being secondary to and dependent on them, and adapt yourselves to them], so that even if any do not obey the Word [of God], they may be won over not by discussion but by the [godly] lives of their wives, 2 When they observe the pure and modest way in which you conduct yourselves, together with your reverence [for your husband; you are to feel for him all that reverence includes: to respect, defer to, revere him — to honor, esteem, appreciate, prize, and, in the human sense, to adore him, that is, to admire, praise, be devoted to, deeply love, and enjoy your husband]* AMP

Prov 12:4 *A virtuous and worthy wife [earnest and strong in character] is a crowning joy to her husband.* AMP

Eph 5:23 *For the husband is head of the wife as Christ is the Head of the church...* AMP

Col 3:18 *Wives, be subject to your husbands [subordinate and adapt yourselves to them], as is right and fitting and your proper duty in the Lord.* AMP

Prov 5:18 *Let your fountain [of human life] be blessed [with the rewards of fidelity], and rejoice in the wife of your youth.* AMP

Prov 31:12 *She comforts, encourages, and does him only good as long as there is life within her.* AMP

FOUR COMMANDS FOR WIVES FROM EPHESIANS 5

1. Be submissive to your husband...v. 22
2. Recognize your husband's headship...v. 23
3. Be subject to your husband in everything...v. 24
4. Respect and reverence your husband...v. 33

THE CHILDREN

Children under the age of accountability to God are saved (Matt 18:1-10). That age is unknown and would vary from child to child. It is certain, from that age on, each child has a choice to make. "As for me and my house, we will serve the Lord."

Prov 22:6 *Train up a child in the way he should go [and in keeping with his individual gift or bent], and when he is old he will not depart from it.* AMP

Prov 22:15 *Foolishness is bound up in the heart of a child, but the rod of discipline will drive it far from him.* AMP

Prov 20:20 *Whoever curses his father or his mother, his lamp shall be put out in complete darkness.* AMP

Prov 29:15 *The rod and reproof give wisdom, but a child left undisciplined brings his mother to shame.* AMP

Titus 2:4 *So that they will wisely train the young women to be sane and sober of mind (temperate, disciplined) and to love their husbands and their children...* AMP

Eph 6:1-3 *CHILDREN, OBEY your parents in the Lord [as His representatives], for this is just and right. 2 Honor (esteem and value as precious) your father and your mother — this is the first commandment with a promise. 3 That all may be well with you and that you may live long on the earth.* AMP

Luke 1:80 *And the little boy grew and became strong in spirit;* AMP

Prov 23:13 *Withhold not discipline from the child; for if you strike and punish him with the [reedlike] rod, he will not die.* AMP

God's promises for your children

Jer 31:16-17 *Thus says the Lord, "Restrain your voice from weeping And your eyes*
from tears. For your work will be rewarded," declares the Lord, "And they will return from the land of the enemy. 17 "There is hope for your future," declares the Lord, "And your children will return to their own territory..."

Isa 54:13
All your sons will be taught of the Lord; And the well-being of your sons will be great.

Prov 11:21 *... the descendants of the righteous will be delivered.*

Ps 112:1-2 *Praise the Lord! How blessed is the man who fears the Lord, Who greatly delights in His commandments. 2 His descendants will be mighty on earth; The generation of the upright will be blessed.*

Isa 49:25 *...I will save your sons.*

Ps 145:9-10 *The Lord is good to all, And His mercies are over all His works. 10 All Your works shall give thanks to You, O Lord, And Your godly ones shall bless You.*

Isa 44:3-4 *I will pour out My Spirit on your offspring And My blessing on your descendants; 4 And they will spring up among the grass Like poplars by streams of water.*

Isa 59:21 *As for Me, this is My covenant with them," says the Lord: "My Spirit which is upon you, and My words which I have put in your mouth shall not depart from your mouth, nor from the mouth of your offspring, nor from the mouth of your offspring's offspring," says the Lord, "from now and forever."*

DIVORCE

This topic is very difficult to draw conclusions. Below are the Scriptures that directly address the issue.

Matt 5:31-32 *It has also been said, Whoever divorces his wife must give her a certificate of divorce. 32 But I tell you, Whoever dismisses and repudiates and divorces his wife, except on the grounds of unfaithfulness (sexual immorality), causes her to commit adultery, and whoever marries a woman who has been divorced commits adultery.* AMP

Luke 16:18 *Whoever divorces (dismisses and repudiates) his wife and marries another commits adultery, and he who marries a woman who is divorced from her husband commits adultery.* AMP

Matt 19:4-10 *He replied, Have you never read that He Who made them from the beginning made them male and female, 5 And said, For this reason a man shall leave his father and mother and shall be united firmly (joined inseparably) to his wife, and the two shall become one flesh? [Gen 1:27; 2:24.] 6 So they are no longer two, but one flesh. What therefore God has joined together, let not man put asunder (separate). 7 They said to Him, Why then did Moses command [us] to give a certificate of divorce and thus to dismiss and repudiate a wife? [Deut 24:1-4.]*
8 He said to them, Because of the hardness (stubbornness and perversity) of your hearts Moses permitted you to dismiss and repudiate and divorce your wives; but from the beginning it has not been so [ordained]. 9 I say to you: whoever dismisses (repudiates, divorces) his wife, except for unchastity, and marries another commits adultery, and he who marries a divorced woman commits adultery. 10 The disciples said to Him, If the case of a man with his wife is like this, it is neither profitable nor advisable to marry. AMP

1 Cor 7:10-11 *But to the married people I give charge — not I but the Lord — that the wife is not to separate from her husband. 11 But if she does [separate from and divorce him], let her remain single or else be reconciled to her husband. And [I charge] the husband [also] that he should not put away or divorce his wife.* AMP

Mark 10:9 *What therefore God has united (joined together), let not man separate or divide.* AMP
      (also see Mark 10:2-11)
The law concerning the subject in the Old Testament is found in Deut 24:1-4; Jesus referred to this in Matt 5 and Luke 16)

FASTING

(The Bible records 35 fasts)

Est 4:16 *Go, gather together all the Jews that are present in Shushan, and fast for me; and neither eat nor drink for three days, night or day. I also and my maids will fast as you do.* AMP

Dan 10:3 *I ate no pleasant or desirable food, nor did any meat or wine come into my mouth; and I did not anoint myself at all for the full three weeks.* AMP

Matt 6:16 *And whenever you are fasting, do not look gloomy and sour and dreary like the hypocrites, for they put on a dismal countenance, that their fasting may be apparent to and seen by men. Truly I say to you, they have their reward in full already.* AMP

Matt 9:15 *...when the bridegroom is taken away from them, and then they will fast.* AMP

Joel 2:15 *Blow the trumpet in Zion; set apart a fast [a day of restraint and humility].* AMP

Acts 13:2 *While they were worshiping the Lord and fasting...* AMP

Ezra 8:23 *So we fasted and besought our God for this, and He heard our entreaty.* AMP

Jonah 3:5 *So the people of Nineveh believed in God and proclaimed a fast...* AMP

Isa 58:6 *[Rather] is not this the fast that I have chosen: to loose the bonds of wickedness, to undo the bands of the yoke, to let the oppressed go free, and that you break every [enslaving] yoke?* AMP

Ezra 10:6 *...he did not eat bread nor drink water, for he was mourning over the unfaithfulness of the exiles.*

2 Chron 20:3-4 *Then Jehoshaphat feared, and set himself [determinedly, as his vital need] to seek the Lord; he proclaimed a fast in all Judah. 4 And Judah*

gathered together to ask help from the Lord; even out of all the cities of Judah they came to seek the Lord [yearning for Him with all their desire]. AMP
Neh 1:4 *When I heard this, I sat down and wept and mourned for days and fasted and prayed [constantly] before the God of heaven...* AMP

Acts 13:2 *While they were worshiping the Lord and fasting, the Holy Spirit said...* AMP

Most of 35 Bible fasts recorded included prayer. Our pattern should include Declare the fast, Decide the length, Define the purpose, and Determine to complete the fast, with prayer, In Jesus Name.

*F*AVOR AND *H*ONOR

A STUDY

GOD IS A GOD OF FAVOR (GRACE)

Ps 86:15 *But You, O Lord, are a God merciful and gracious, slow to anger and abounding in mercy and loving-kindness and truth.* AMP

Ps 103:5 *The Lord is compassionate and gracious, Slow to anger and abounding in lovingkindness.*

GOD GIVES FAVOR Num 6:25 *The Lord make His face shine on you, And be gracious to you;*

Zech 12:10 *"I will pour out on the house of David and on the inhabitants of Jerusalem, the Spirit of grace..."*

Luke 2:40 *The Child continued to grow and become strong, increasing in wisdom; and the grace of God was upon Him.*

Luke 2:52 *And Jesus kept increasing in wisdom and stature, and in favor with God and men.*

1 Sam 2:26 *Now the boy Samuel was growing in stature and in favor both with the Lord and with men.*

Ps 8:5 *And You crown him with glory and majesty!*

John 17:22 *And the glory which You gave Me I have given them, that they may be one just as We are one...* NKJV

GOD FAVORS AND HONORS THOSE THAT LOVE HIM

Eph 6:24 *Grace (God's undeserved favor) be with all who love our Lord Jesus Christ with undying and incorruptible [love]. Amen (so let it be).* AMP

Prov 12:2 *A good man obtains favor from the Lord, but a man of wicked devices He condemns.* AMP

Ps 84:11 *For the Lord God is a Sun and Shield; the Lord bestows [present] grace and favor and [future] glory (honor, splendor, and heavenly bliss)! No good thing will He withhold from those who walk uprightly.* AMP

Ps 5:12 *For it is You who blesses the righteous man, O Lord, You surround him with favor as with a shield.*

John 12:26 *...if anyone serves Me the Father will honor him.*

GOD FAVORS ME AS I HONOR HIS WORD
Prov 8:35 *"For he who finds me finds life And obtains favor from the Lord."*

Josh 1:8-9 *"This book of the law shall not depart from your mouth, but you shall meditate on it day and night, so that you may be careful to do according to all that is written in it; for then you will make your way prosperous, and then you will have success.*

Ps 1:1-3 *How blessed is the man who does not walk in the counsel of the wicked, Nor stand in the path of sinners, Nor sit in the seat of scoffers! 2 But his delight is in the law of the Lord, And in His law he meditates day and night. 3 He will be like a tree firmly planted by streams of water, Which yields its fruit in its season And its leaf does not wither; And in whatever he does, he prospers.*

GOD FAVORS THOSE WHO SEEK HIM
Jer 33:2 *'Call to Me and I will answer you, and I will tell you great and mighty things, which you do not know.'*

Ps 34:10 *Even strong young lions sometimes go hungry, but those of us who reverence the Lord will never lack any good thing...* TLB

Matt 6:33 *But seek (aim at and strive after) first of all His kingdom and His righteousness (His way of doing and being right), and then all these things taken together will be given you besides.* AMP

Prov 3:3-4 *Let not mercy and truth forsake you; Bind them around your neck, Write them on the tablet of your heart, 4 And so find favor and high esteem In the sight of God and man.* NKJV

WE MUST PLANT FAVOR IN ORDER TO RECEIVE IT

Gal 6:7 *Do not be deceived, God is not mocked; for whatever a man sows, that he will also reap.* NKJV

GOD BRINGS US INTO FAVOR WITH GOD AND MAN

Dan 1:9 *Now God granted Daniel favor and compassion in the sight of the commander of the officials.*

Gen 39:4 *So Joseph found favor in his sight and became his personal servant; and he made him overseer over his house, and all that he owned he put in his charge*

Est 2:15-16 *Now when the turn of Esther, the daughter of Abihail the uncle of Mordecai who had taken her as his daughter, came to go in to the king, she did not request anything except what Hegai, the king's eunuch who was in charge of the women, advised. And Esther found favor in the eyes of all who saw her.*

Est 2:17 *The king loved Esther more than all the other women, and she obtained grace and favor in his sight.* NKJV

Ex 3:21 *And I will give this people favor in the sight of the Egyptians;* NKJV

*F*EAR

A STUDY

"Don't give fear the power to make you fearful."

2 Tim 1:7 *For God has not given us a spirit of fear, but of power and of love and of a sound mind.* NKJV

Rom 8:15 *For you have not received a spirit of slavery leading to fear again...*

Jer 1:8 *"Do not be afraid of them, For I am with you to deliver you," declares the Lord.*

Neh 4:14 *I looked [them over] and rose up and said to the nobles and officials and the other people, Do not be afraid of the enemy; [earnestly] remember the Lord and imprint Him [on your minds]...* AMP

WHAT FEAR WILL DO

Fear brings the enemy
Prov 29:25 *The fear of man brings a snare, But whoever trusts in the Lord shall be safe.* NKJV

Job 3:25 *For the thing I greatly feared has come upon me, And what I dreaded has happened to me.* NKJV

Prov 10:24 *The fear of the wicked will come upon him,* NKJV

Ps 105:38 *...the fear of them had fallen upon them.* NKJV

It is very clear, the thing which you fear, will probably park in your living room tonight!

Fear will spread and weaken a group
Deut 20:8-9 *"The officers shall speak further to the people, and say, 'What man is there who is fearful and fainthearted? Let him go and return to his house, lest the heart of his brethren faint like his heart.'"* NKJV

Fear will steal your battle of faith

2 Tim 1:7 *For God has not given us a spirit of fear, but of power and of love and of a sound mind.* NKJV

Judg 7:3 *Whoever is fearful and afraid, let him turn and depart...* NKJV

Fear will destroy you!

Deut 28:60-61 *He will bring back on you all the diseases of Egypt, of which you were afraid, and they shall cling to you.* NKJV

Jer 42:16 *...the sword which you feared shall overtake you.* NKJV

Prov 29:25 *The fear of man brings a snare...* AMP

HOW TO DESTROY FEAR

You DECIDE to remove it from your spirit

Ps 118:6 *The Lord is on my side; I will not fear.* NKJV

Ps 56:4 *In God (I will praise His word), In God I have put my trust; I will not fear. What can flesh do to me?* NKJV

John 14:27 *Peace I leave with you; My [own] peace I now give and bequeath to you. Not as the world gives do I give to you. Do not let your hearts be troubled, neither let them be afraid. [Stop allowing yourselves to be agitated and disturbed; and do not permit yourselves to be fearful and intimidated and cowardly and unsettled.]* AMP

Ps 3:6 *I will not be afraid of ten thousands of people who have set themselves against me round about.* AMP

Fear is overcome by joy (*also refer to JOY study*)

Phil 4:4-5 *Rejoice in the Lord always; again I will say, rejoice!*

1 Thess 5:18 *... in everything give thanks; for this is God's will for you in Christ Jesus.*

Josh 6:20 *So the people shouted, and priests blew the trumpets; and when the people heard the sound of the trumpet, the people shouted with a great shout and the wall fell down flat...*

Always remember Satan's program is fed by fear. His program is destroyed by joy and positive faith. Fear is to Satan as Faith is to god.

"Fear is overcome with faith in God."

Rom 8:15-16 *For you have not received a spirit of slavery leading to fear again, but you have received a spirit of adoption as sons by which we cry out, "Abba! Father!"*

Ps 34:4 *I sought (inquired of) the Lord and required Him [of necessity and on the authority of His Word], and He heard me, and delivered me from all my fears.* AMP

Ps 27:1 *The Lord is my light and my salvation; Whom shall I fear?* NKJV

Phil 1:28 *...in no way alarmed by your opponents*

Isa 35:3-4 *Encourage the exhausted, and strengthen the feeble. 4 Say to those with anxious heart, "Take courage, fear not. Behold, your God will come with vengeance..."*

Eph 6:10 *Finally, be strong in the Lord and in the strength of His might.*

Luke 1:30, *The angel said to her, "Do not be afraid,...may it be done to me according to your word.*

Luke 12:32 *Do not be seized with alarm and struck with fear...* AMP

Eph 3:12 *In Whom, because of our faith in Him, we dare to have the boldness (courage and confidence) of free access (an unreserved approach to God with freedom and without fear).* AMP

Isa 14:3 *When the Lord has given you rest from your sorrow and pain and from your trouble and unrest and from the hard service with which you were made to serve...* AMP

Mark 4:40 *He said to them, Why are you so timid and fearful? How is it that you have no faith...* AMP

Fear is overcome by love
1 John 4:18There is no fear in love [dread does not exist], but full-grown (complete,
 perfect) love turns fear out of doors and expels every trace of terror. AMP

Fear is overcome by looking to Jesus, not the problem
Heb 12:2 ... *fixing our eyes on Jesus, the author and perfecter of faith...*

Deut 20:1-2 *"When you go out to battle against your enemies and see horses and chariots and people more numerous than you, do not be afraid of them; for the Lord your God, who brought you up from the land of Egypt, is with you..."*

2 Chron 20:15-16 *...thus says the Lord to you, 'Do not fear or be dismayed because of this great multitude, for the battle is not yours but God's.*

Prov 1:33 *But whoever listens to me will dwell safely, And will be secure, without fear of evil.* NKJV

SEVEN THINGS NOT TO FEAR:

1. **Flesh**; Ps 56:4 In God *(I will praise His word)*, In God I have put my trust; I will not fear. What can flesh do to me? NKJV

2. **People**; Num 14:9 *...do not rebel against the Lord, nor fear the people of the land...*NKJV

3. **Idols**; Judg 6:10 "I am the Lord your God; do not fear the gods of the Amorites..." NKJV

   2 Kings 17:35-36 *"You shall not fear other gods, nor bow down to them nor serve them nor sacrifice to them..."* NKJV

4. **Evil**; Ps 23:4
   Yea, though I walk through the valley of the shadow of death, I will fear no evil; NKJV

5. **War**; Ps 27:3 *Though an army may encamp against me, My heart shall not fear...* NKJV

6. **Man;** Luke 12:5 *But I will show you whom you should fear: Fear Him who, after He has killed, has power to cast into hell; yes, I say to you, fear Him!*
   NKJV

7. **Suffering**; Rev 2:10 *Do not fear any of those things which you are about to suffer.* NKJV

Mark 5:36-37 *But Jesus, overhearing what was being spoken, said to the synagogue official, "Do not be afraid any longer, only believe."*

FORGIVE

(See below, how to overcome UNFORGIVENESS, a positive attitude and confession)

Matt 6:14-15 *For if you forgive others for their transgressions, your heavenly Father will also forgive you. 15 But if you do not forgive others, then your Father will not forgive your transgressions.*

Matt 18:15 *If your brother sins, go and show him his fault in private; if he listens to you, you have won your brother.*

Mark 11:25 *Whenever you stand praying, forgive, if you have anything against anyone, so that your Father who is in heaven will also forgive you your transgressions.*

Col 3:13-14 *...bearing with one another, and forgiving each other, whoever has a complaint against anyone; just as the Lord forgave you, so also should you.*

Eph 4:32 *Be kind to one another, tender-hearted, forgiving each other, just as God in Christ also has forgiven you.*

Luke 17:4 *And if he sins against you seven times a day, and returns to you seven times, saying, 'I repent,' forgive him.*

Neh 9:17 *But You are a God of forgiveness, Gracious and compassionate...*

John 20:23 *[Now having received the Holy Spirit and being led and directed by Him] if you forgive the sins of anyone, they are forgiven; if you retain the sins of anyone, they are retained.* AMP

Matt 5:22 *But I say to you that everyone who continues to be angry with his brother or harbors malice (enmity of heart) against him shall be liable to and unable to escape the punishment imposed by the court 24 Leave your gift at the altar and go. First make peace with your brother, and then come back and present your gift.* AMP

Matt 18:21-22 *Then Peter came to Him and said, "Lord, how often shall my brother sin against me, and I forgive him? Up to seven times?" 22 Jesus said to him, "I do not say to you, up to seven times, but up to seventy times seven.* NKJV

UNFORGIVENESS, a positive attitude and declaration

Each of us at times, have experienced some unforgiveness. Perhaps someone treated you unfairly? A coworker or even friend said something that came back to you in conversation. Deal with it right then. Here is a personal confession of faith. I am not the author but copied it down many years ago. I give my appreciation to the unknown originator of this positive attitude to speak forth.

Also, know that what you confess you'll possess. When you say what God says about any subject or topic, you will possess what He has provided for you. Concerning the vital subject of unforgiveness, you'll possess what He has provided for you: the divine ability to forgive everyone and walk in peace.

Say it:

1. "If I forgive men their trespasses against me, my heavenly Father will also forgive me my trespasses against Him (Matthew 6: 14). But if I forgive not men their trespasses against me. far more serious consequences than I had imagined will he mine and *your Father will not forgive your transgressions.* V. 15.

2. "If I possess unforgiveness in my heart towards others regardless of their wrong doings against me, I open my heart to permit seven other spirits more wicked than unforgiveness to enter in (Luke 11:26). Here are seven other spirits which are akin to unforgiveness but are even more wicked:
   - *a.* Resentment
   - *b.* Ill-will
   - *c.* A grudge
   - *d.* Malice
   - *e.* Retaliation
   - *f.* Bitterness
   - *g.* Hatred

3. "As I examine this list of seven other spirits more wicked than unforgiveness. I perceive that they are progressively degrading. How can I be delivered from unforgiveness? How can I resist these wrong spirits in Jesus' name, that they must leave me? I can *be kind to each other, tenderhearted, forgiving one another, just as God has forgiven (me)* TLB. Kindness is a fruit of the Spirit, which when coupled with tenderheartedness, enables me to forgive all who have wronged me, even as God for Christ's sake has forgiven me.

4. "If I have a quarrel with anyone. I must forgive him. Even as Christ has forgiven me. I also forgive others (Colossians 3: 13). God's Word is so practical and powerful: it shows me what to do even if I should be involved in a petty quarrel.

5. "God's ability within me to forgive others is unlimited. Jesus has commanded me to forgive even "seventy times seven" times, meaning that I possess, not natural ability, but supernatural ability, whereby I can forgive others.

6. "The greatest problems I encounter in fife may well be "people problems." I live in a world where communications can break" down; fellowship may be severed; persecution and opposition may be my lot. But I know the secret. I have the ability to love with God's love. H is love will enable me to see others through eyes of tender love and compassion.

7. "I refuse to speak unkindly against those who have wronged me. God enables me to forgive and to forget. 'Seven other spirits' may often seek to gain entrance to my life, but I defiantly resist them in Jesus' name!

8. "Some say, 'I would forgive others if they would only ask me for forgiveness.' Whether they ever ask for forgiveness or not, in my heart I forgive and put all offenses under the Blood of Jesus. As a person who follows Jesus, I forgive others. By the delivering power of the Blood of Jesus', I am free from 'seven other spirits.'"

*F*REE

A STUDY

NATURE OF GOD

Isa 58:6 *"Is not this the kind of fasting I have chosen: to loose the chains of injustice and untie the cords of the yoke, to set the oppressed free and break every yoke?* NIV

Jer 34:17 *'Behold, I am proclaiming a release to you,' declares the Lord...*

Rom 8:32 *He who did not spare His own Son, but delivered Him over for us all, how will He not also with Him freely give us all things?*

1 Cor 2:12 *Now we have received, not the spirit of the world, but the Spirit who is from God, so that we may know the things freely given to us by God...*

Rev 22:17 *...let the one who is thirsty come; let the one who wishes take the water of life without cost.*

SET FREE BY JESUS

John 8:36 *So if the Son makes you free, you will be free indeed.*

Luke 4:18 *"THE SPIRIT OF THE LORD IS UPON ME,*
BECAUSE HE ANOINTED ME TO PREACH THE GOSPEL TO THE POOR.
HE HAS SENT ME TO PROCLAIM RELEASE TO THE CAPTIVES,
AND RECOVERY OF SIGHT TO THE BLIND,
TO SET FREE THOSE WHO ARE OPPRESSED..."

Gal 5:1 *IN [this] freedom Christ has made us free [and completely liberated us]; stand fast then, and do not be hampered and held ensnared and submit again to a yoke of slavery [which you have once put off].* AMP

Gal 2:4 *...false brethren secretly brought in, who had sneaked in to spy out our liberty which we have in Christ Jesus, in order to bring us into bondage.*

Rom 8:2 *For the law of the Spirit of life in Christ Jesus has set you free from the law of sin and of death.*

John 8:32 *...And you shall know the truth, and the truth shall make you free.* NKJV

MAN CREATED TO BE FREE

Gen 1:26 *Let Us make man in Our image, according to Our likeness; let them have dominion over the fish of the sea, over the birds of the air, and over the cattle, over all the earth and over every creeping thing that creeps on the earth...* NKJV

Gen 1:28 *Then God blessed them, and God said to them, "Be fruitful and multiply; fill the earth and subdue it..."* NKJV

Gen 2:15 *And the Lord God took the man and put him in the Garden of Eden to tend and guard and keep it.* AMP

Gen 2:16 *And the Lord God commanded the man, saying, You may freely eat of every tree of the garden...* AMP

Gen 2:19 *...and whatever Adam called every living creature, that was its name.* AMP

A BELIEVER IS TO EXERCISE HIS FREEDOM

2 Chron 29:31 *...and as many as were of a willing heart brought burnt offerings.* AMP

Acts 3:8 *And leaping forth he stood and began to walk, and he went into the temple with them, walking and leaping and praising God.* AMP

FRIEND

Judg 14:20 *...his companion who had been his friend.*

James 2:23 *...and he was called the friend of God.*

Prov 18:24 *But there is a friend who sticks closer than a brother.*

Ps 41:9 *Even my close friend in whom I trusted...*

Ps 14:5 There they shall be in great fear, for God is with the generation of the righteous. AMP

Ps 103;17-18 But the mercy and loving kindness of the Lord are from everlasting to everlasting upon those who...fear Him and His righteousness is to children's children. To such as keep His covenant, hearing receiving and obeying it; and to those who remember His commandments to do them. AMP

Ps 105:8 He is mindful of His covenant and forever (it is imprinted on His heart), the word which He commanded and established to a thousand generations. AMP

Ps 33:11 The counsel of the Lord stands forever, the thoughts of His heart to all generations. AMP

Ps 100:5 For the Lord is good; His mercy and lovingkindness are everlasting; His faithfulness and truth endure to all generations. AMP

Pro 13:22 A good man leaves an inheritance to his children's' children and the wealth of the sinner (finds its way eventually) into the hands of the righteous, for whom it was laid up. AMP

Ps 119:90 Your faithfulness is from generation to generation; You have established the earth, and it stands fast. AMP

Isa 59:21 ....and my words which I have put in your mouth shall not depart out of your mouth, or out of the mouth of your children, or out of the mouth of your children's children, from henceforth and forever. AMP   *skh. 1983*

GIVING
A STUDY

GOD RETURNS THAT WHICH WE GIVE

Prov 19:17 *One who is gracious to a poor man lends to the Lord, And He will repay him for his good deed.*

Prov 28:27 *He who gives to the poor will never want, But he who shuts his eyes willhave many curses.*

Eccl 11:1-2 *Cast your bread on the surface of the waters, for you will find it after many days.*

Matt 10:42 *And whoever in the name of a disciple gives to one of these little ones even a cup of cold water to drink, truly I say to you, he shall not lose his reward.*

Mark 10:28-30 *Peter began to say to Him, "Behold, we have left everything and followed You." 29 Jesus said, "Truly I say to you, there is no one who has left house or brothers or sisters or mother or father or children or farms, for My sake and for the gospel's sake, 30 but that he will receive a hundred times as much now in the present age, houses and brothers and sisters and mothers and children and farms, along with persecutions; and in the age to come, eternal life.*

2 Cor 9:6-7 *Now this I say, he who sows sparingly will also reap sparingly, and he who sows bountifully will also reap bountifully. 7 Each one must do just as he has purposed in his heart, not grudgingly or under compulsion, for God loves a cheerful giver.*

Prov 11:24 *There is one who scatters, and yet increases all the more, And there is one who withholds what is justly due, and yet it results only in want.*

Prov 3:9-10 *Honor the Lord from your wealth And from the first of all your produce;*
10 So your barns will be filled with plenty And your vats will overflow with new wine.

Mark 4:24-25 *And He was saying to them, "Take care what you listen to. By your standard of measure it will be measured to you; and more will be given you besides. 25 For whoever has, to him more shall be given; and whoever does not have, even what he has shall be taken away from him."*

Luke 6:38 *Give, and it will be given to you. They will pour into your lap a good measure—pressed down, shaken together, and running over. For by your standard of measure it will be measured to you in return.*

GIVE TO YOUR LOCAL CHURCH BODY---GOD'S TITHE + YOUR OFFERINGS

BEFORE THE LAW
Gen 14:19 *And [Abram] gave him a tenth of all [he had taken].* AMP

Gen 28:22 *...of all [the increase of possessions] that You give me I will give the tenth to You.* AMP

Heb 7:2 *And Abraham gave to him a tenth portion of all...* AMP

Heb 7:6 *...received tithes from Abraham [himself] and blessed him who possessed the promises [of God].* AMP

UNDER THE LAW
Mal 3:10 *Bring all the tithes (the whole tenth of your income) into the storehouse, that there may be food in My house, and prove Me now by it, says the Lord of hosts, if I will not open the windows of heaven for you and pour you out a blessing, that there shall not be room enough to receive it.* AMP

Neh 10:32 *Also we pledge ourselves to pay yearly a third of a shekel for the service expenses of the house of our God [which are]...* AMP

Heb 7:5 *And those indeed of the sons of Levi who receive the priest's office have commandment in the Law to collect a tenth from the people...*

Deut 14:28 *At the end of every third year you shall bring out all the tithe of your produce in that year, and shall deposit it in your town*

Prov 3:9 *Honor the Lord from your wealth And from the first of all your produce...*

Lev 27:31-33 ...If, therefore, a man wishes to redeem part of his tithe, he shall add to it one-fifth of it. 32 'For every tenth part of herd or flock, whatever passes under the rod, the tenth one shall be holy to the Lord.

Neh 12:44 On that day men were also appointed over the chambers for the stores,
the contributions, the first fruits and the tithes

NEW TESTAMENT
Matt 23:23 Woe to you, scribes and Pharisees, pretenders (hypocrites)! For you give a tenth of your mint and dill and cummin, and have neglected and omitted the weightier (more important) matters of the Law... AMP

1 Cor 16:2 On the first [day] of each week, let each one of you [personally] put aside something and save it up as he has prospered [in proportion to what he is given]... AMP

Luke 18:12 I fast twice a week; I give tithes of all that I gain. AMP

Rom 12:13 Contribute to the needs of God's people [sharing in the necessities of the saints]... AMP

EXAMPLES OF PAYING TITHE
Abraham (Gen 14:20; Heb 7:1-11)
Nehemiah and Israel (Neh 13)
Jacob (Gen 28:22)
Hypocrites (Matt 23:23; Lk 11:42; 18:12)
Levi through Abraham (Heb 7:9)
Hezekiah and Israel (2 Chr 31)
Christians (1 Cor 9:7-14; 16:2; 2 Cor 7:11; 8:1-15; Gal 6:6; 1   Tim
                5:17-18 ; Heb 7)

GIVE TO THOSE IN NEED
Ps 112:9 He has distributed freely [he has given to the poor and needy]... AMP

Prov 19:17 He who has pity on the poor lends to the Lord, and that which he has given He will repay to him. AMP

Prov 28:27 He who gives to the poor will not want... AMP

Rom 12:13 *Contribute to the needs of God's people [sharing in the necessities of the saints]; pursue the practice of hospitality.* AMP

GIVE TO THE MINISTRY... THOSE WHO SPIRITUALLY FEED YOU
Gal 6:6 *Let him who receives instruction in the Word [of God] share all good things with his teacher [contributing to his support].* AMP

Isa 23:18 *Yet her profit and her earnings will be set apart for the Lord; they will not be stored up or hoarded. Her profits will go to those who live before the Lord, for abundant food and fine clothes.* NIV

Deut 26:12-13 *When you have finished setting aside a tenth of all your produce in the third year, the year of the tithe, you shall give it to the Levite, the alien, the fatherless and the widow, so that they may eat in your towns and be satisfied.* NIV

Neh 10:37 *Moreover, we will bring to the storerooms of the house of our God, to the priests, the first of our ground meal, of our [grain] offerings, of the fruit of all our trees and of our new wine and oil. And we will bring a tithe of our crops to the Levites, for it is the Levites who collect the tithes in all the towns where we work.* NIV

GIVE SACRIFICIALLY
Mark 12:42-44 *But a poor widow came and put in two very small copper coins, worth only a fraction of a penny. 43 Calling his disciples to him, Jesus said, "I tell you the truth, this poor widow has put more into the treasury than all the others. 44 They all gave out of their wealth; but she, out of her poverty, put in everything — all she had to live on."* NIV

1 Kings 17:13 *Elijah said to her, "Don't be afraid. Go home and do as you have said. But first make a small cake of bread for me from what you have and bring it to me, and then make something for yourself and your son...* NIV

A POSITIVE DECLARATION AFTER YOU GIVE

God will do what He declares. You are affirming it so.

1. I have proven God with tithes and offerings according to Malachi 3, and I now know that God will open the windows of heaven unto me and pour out an overflowing blessing that there will not be room enough to receive. I am praising Him for opening heaven's windows to my soul and for His abundant blessing that makes rich and adds no sorrow. Make this a personal affirmation of God's Word. God will do what He says.

2. Further, I know God has promised, in response to my loving' obedience in giving, that He will rebuke the devourer for my sake. The devil is the devourer who would' devour' my finances, the harmony of my home, my peace of mind. I praise the Lord that He is rebuking the devourer for my sake!

3. I know that God is supplying all my needs according to His riches in glory by Christ Jesus. I shall hold fast to this confession without wavering. James 1:7 declares that men who waver will not receive anything from the Lord. But I will not waver in my expectations that God will open heaven's windows, pouring out the blessings that there will not be room enough to receive, and that He's rebuking the devourer for my sake. It is being done, hallelujah!

4. I have' sown bountifully, so God declares that I shall reap bountifully. Bountiful blessings financially are mine because God says so, and God is not a man that He should lie.

5.   I have given not grudgingly nor of necessity. I have given cheerfully because "God loveth a cheerful giver" (2

Corinthians 9:7). I know that if I were, to withhold from God that it would tend to poverty (Proverbs 11:24). But I practice liberality in my giving and thereby He ministers to all my needs.

6. I am discovering the reality of the words of Jesus that it is more blessed to give than to receive (Acts 20:35). To be a cheerful, hilarious giver (2 Corinthians 9:7), is the source of tremendous blessing, even greater than receiving. But as I give the Lord just sees to it that it's given unto me, good measure, pressed down, and shaken together and running over shall men given unto my bosom (see Luke 6:38).

7. God's Word is His great "anti-poverty plan" to keep me in abundance of money and material possessions, to meet the needs of my family, and most of all, to give to the advancing of His Gospel world-wide.

Glory

A STUDY

In studying The Glory of God, there seems to be two distinct manifestations. (1) the actual glory that God is, which is seldom, if ever seen. It is God manifesting Himself in a powerful, and many times visible form. (On the mountain with Moses, the "burning bush" earlier in Moses' life, appearance of Jesus, etc. See Scriptures below). (2) His glory is an honor that believers have been given and are to ascribe back to Him in praise and attention. We have, to some extent, both of these today in healings, miracles, and joy overflowing from His presence.

Three Stages of a Believers Progressive Growth in Glory
1. A worship from the heart
2. Healings, miracles, overflowing joy
3. Glory

Hab 2:14 *But [the time is coming when] the earth shall be filled with the knowledge of the glory of the Lord as the waters cover the sea.* AMP

2 Cor 4:6 *For God Who said, Let light shine out of darkness, has shone in our hearts so as [to beam forth] the Light for the illumination of the knowledge of the majesty and glory of God.* AMP

Isa 60:1 *ARISE [from the depression and prostration in which circumstances have kept you — rise to a new life]! Shine (be radiant with the glory of the Lord), for your light has come, and the glory of the Lord has risen upon you!* AMP

Isa 35:2 *They shall see the glory of the Lord, the majesty and splendor and excellency of our God.* AMP

HIS GLORY DESCRIBED

Matt 17:2 *And His appearance underwent a change in their presence; and His face shone clear and bright like the sun, and His clothing became as white as light.* AMP

Rev 1:14 *His head and His hair were white like white wool, [as white] as snow, and His eyes [flashed] like a flame of fire.* AMP

Dan 7:9 *I kept looking until thrones were placed [for the assessors with the Judge], and the Ancient of Days [God, the eternal Father] took His seat, Whose garment was white as snow and the hair of His head like pure wool. His throne was like the fiery flame; its wheels were burning fire.* AMP

Deut 33:2 *He said, The Lord came from Sinai and beamed upon us from Seir; He flashed forth from Mount Paran, from among ten thousands of holy ones, a flaming fir.* AMP

Ps 104:2 *[You are the One] Who covers Yourself with light as with a garment...* AMP

Hab 3:4 *And His brightness was like the sunlight; rays streamed from His hand, and there [in the sun like splendor] was the hiding place of His power.* AMP

Ezek 1:28 *Like the appearance of the bow that is in the cloud on the day of rain, so was the appearance of the brightness round about. This was the appearance of the likeness of the glory of the Lord. And when I saw it, I fell upon my face and I heard a voice of One speaking.* AMP

Acts 9:3 *Now as he traveled on, he came near to Damascus, and suddenly a light from heaven flashed around him...* AMP

Ex 24:17 *And the glory of the Lord appeared to the Israelites like devouring fire on the top of the mountain.* AMP

Luke 2:9 *And behold, an angel of the Lord stood by them, and the glory of the Lord flashed and shone all about them.* AMP

Acts 7:55 *But he, full of the Holy Spirit and controlled by Him, gazed into heaven and saw the glory (the splendor and majesty) of God, and Jesus standing at God's right hand;* AMP

Ex 16:7, 10 And in the morning, you shall see the glory of the Lord...10 And as Aaron spoke to the whole congregation of Israel, they looked toward the wilderness, and behold, the glory of the Lord appeared in the cloud! AMP

Ex 40:34-35 *Then the cloud [the Shekinah, God's visible presence] covered the Tent of Meeting, and the glory of the Lord filled the tabernacle! [Rev 15:8.] 35*

And Moses was not able to enter the Tent of Meeting because the cloud remained upon it, and the glory of the Lord filled the tabernacle. AMP

Lev 9:5 *And Moses said, This is the thing which the Lord commanded you to do, and the glory of the Lord will appear to you.* AMP

Num 16:42 *When the congregation was gathered against Moses and Aaron, they looked at the Tent of Meeting, and behold, the cloud covered it and they saw the Lord's glory.* AMP

Num 20:6 *Then Moses and Aaron went from the presence of the assembly to the door of the Tent of Meeting and fell on their faces. Then the glory of the Lord appeared to them.* AMP

1 Kings 8:10-11 *When the priests had come out of the Holy Place, the cloud filled the Lord's house, 11 So the priests could not stand to minister because of the cloud, for the glory of the Lord had filled the Lord's house.* AMP

2 Chron 5:13-14 *And when the trumpeters and singers were joined in unison, making one sound to be heard in praising and thanking the Lord, and when they lifted up their voice with the trumpets and cymbals and other instruments for song and praised the Lord, saying, For He is good, for His mercy and loving-kindness endure forever, then the house of the Lord was filled with a cloud, 14 So that the priests could not stand to minister because of the cloud, for the glory of the Lord filled the house of God.* AMP

2 Chron 7:1-2 *WHEN SOLOMON had finished praying, the fire came down from heaven and consumed the burnt offering and the sacrifices, and the glory of the Lord filled the house. 2 The priests could not enter the house of the Lord, because the glory of the Lord had filled the Lord's house.* AMP

Ezek 3:23 *Then I arose and went forth into the plain, and behold, the glory of the Lord stood there* AMP

When God said "Light...Be!" (this is the way the Hebrew reads), He uncovered Himself, revealed Himself to His extension of Heaven, earth. Adam and Eve walked in that glory. No need for a sun or moon to give light until later.

HIS GLORY UPON US

Eph 1:17-18 *[For I always pray to] the God of our Lord Jesus Christ, the Father of glory, that He may grant you a spirit of wisdom and revelation [of insight into mysteries and secrets] in the [deep and intimate] knowledge of Him, 18 By having the eyes of your heart flooded with light, so that you can know and understand the hope to which He has called you, and how rich is His glorious inheritance in the saints (His set-apart ones)...* AMP

Psalm 29 all verses

2 Cor 4:6 *For God Who said, Let light shine out of darkness, has shone in our hearts so as [to beam forth] the Light for the illumination of the knowledge of the majesty and glory of God.* AMP

Ps 8:5 *Yet You have made him a little lower than God, And You crown him with glory and majesty!*

John 17:22 *"The glory which You have given Me I have given to them..."*

Heb 2:10 *For it was fitting for Him, for whom are all things, and through whom are all things, in bringing many sons to glory...*

2 Thess 2:14 *It was for this He called you through our gospel, that you may gain the glory of our Lord Jesus Christ.*

1 Cor 11:7 *For a man ought not to have his head covered, since he is the image and glory of God...*

Ps 84:11 *For the Lord God is a sun and shield; The Lord gives grace and glory;*

Isa 60:1 *Arise, shine; for your light has come, And the glory of the Lord has risen upon you.*

ALL GLORY IS TO BE GIVEN BACK TO GOD

Eph 3:21 *...to Him be the glory in the church and in Christ Jesus to all generations forever and ever. Amen.*

Matt 5:16 *Let your light shine before men in such a way that they may see your good works, and glorify your Father who is in heaven.*

1 Cor 10:31 *Whether, then, you eat or drink or whatever you do, do all to the glory of God.*

Ps 115:1 *Not to us, O Lord, not to us, But to Your name give glory...*

Isa 43:7 *Everyone who is called by My name, And whom I have created for My glory, Whom I have formed, even whom I have made.*

Eph 1:17 *...the Father of glory...*

Acts 12:23 *...an angel of the Lord struck him because he did not give God the glory,*

Dan 4:31-32 *...King Nebuchadnezzar, to you it is declared: sovereignty has been removed from you, 32 periods of time will pass over you until you recognize that the Most High is ruler over the realm of mankind.*

Acts 14:15-16 *Men, why are you doing these things? We are also men of the same nature as you, and preach the gospel to you that you should turn from these vain things to a living God, WHO MADE THE HEAVEN AND THE EARTH AND THE SEA AND ALL THAT IS IN THEM.*

GOD

(Also refer to the author's NEXT book: *The Essence of Christian Belief*)

"In the beginning God ...." Gen 1:1

ATTRIUTES OF GOD
1. Immortal (1 Tim 1:17)
2. Eternal (1 Tim 1:17)
3. Omnipotent (all powerful, Rev 19:6)
4. Omnipresent (present everywhere, 1 Ki 8:27; Ps 139:7-12)
5. Omniscient (all knowing, Rom 11 :33)
6. Perfect (Deut 32:4; Ps 18:30)
7. Self-existent (Ex 3:14; Jn 1 :4)
8. Holy (Ex 15:11; Isa 6:3)
9. Righteous (Rom 3:21; Heb 12:5-12)
10. Truth (Deut 32:4; Jn 17:3)
11. Love (John 3:16; Rom 15:30)
12. Wisdom (Rom 11:33; 1 Tim 1:17)
13. Merciful (Rom 12:1-2; 2 Cor 1:2)
14. Faithful (1 Cor 10:13; Heb 6:18)

God has always existed: Ps 90:2; 93:2; John 1:1-3; Rev 1:4-8; Deut 29:29

Ten Attributes of God confirmed (Psalm 36)
1. Mercy---high as the heavens
2. Faithfulness---far reaching as the clouds
3. Righteousness---high as mountains
4. Justice--deep as the abyss
5. Preservation---universal as existence
6. Kindness---excellent
7. Providence---complete
8. Satisfaction---rivers of pleasure
9. Life---the fountain of life
10. Light---source of truth

Eighteen Things about God in Psalm 146

1. Man's help in all problems (v. 5)
2. Man's hope of the future life (v. 5)
3. Creator of heaven (v. 6)
4. Creator of earth (v. 6)
5. Creator of the great oceans (v. 6)
6. Creator of all living creatures (v. 6)
7. Keeps truth forever (v. 6)
8. Executes judgment (v. 7)
9. Gives food to the hungry (v. 7)
10. Releases prisoners (v. 7)
11. Raises up those bowed down (v. 8)
12. Opens blind eyes (v. 8)
13. Loves the righteous (v. 8)
14. Preserves strangers (v. 9)
15. Relieves the fatherless and widows (v. 9)
16. Destroys the way of the wicked (v. 9)
17. Reigns forever over man (v. 10)
18. Reigns in Zion over eternal generations (v.10)

Ten Things about God in Psalm 34
1. Sees (v. 15)
2. Hears (vs. 15-16,17)
3. Opposes evil (v. 16)
4. Judges evil (v. 16)
5. Delivers (vs. 17,19)
6. Is near (v. 18)
7. Saves (v. 18)
8. Keeps (v. 29)
9. Redeems (v. 22)
10. Blesses (v. 22)

The works of God's hands:
1. The earth (Ps 8:3, 6)
2. The heavens (Pm 19:1; 102:25)
3. The planets (Isa J0:26; 45:12)
4. All creatures (Gen 2:7-25)
5. All Things (Prov 26:10)

THREE THINGS GOD CANNOT DO
1. Lie (Titus 1:2)
2. Deny Him f (2 Tim 2:13)
3. Be tempted with evil (Jam 1:13)

God changed His mind in Amos 7:3 The Lord changed His mind about this. *"It shall not be," said the Lord.* 7:6 The Lord changed His mind about this. *"This too shall not be," said the Lord God.*

Eight-fold character of Jehovah from Lamentations 3
1. Merciful (v. 22)
2. Compassionate (v. 22)
3. Faithful (vs. 23, 32)
4. Good (v. 25)
5. Deliverer (v. 26)
6. Just and righteous (v. 31)
7. Longsuffering (v. 33)
8. Kind (v. 36)

God is:
Father of Glory (Eph 1:17)
Father of Spirits (Heb 12:9)
Father of Lights (Jam 1:17)
Father of Mercies (2 Cor 1:13)

Eight things God has done for me (Psalm 31)
1. Redeemed me (v. 5) 6.
2. Considers my trouble (v. 7)
3. Knows me in time of adversity (v. 7)
4. Keeps me from enemies (v. 8)
5. Set my feet in a large room (v. 8)
6. Laid up goodness for His own (v. 19)
7. Prepares goodness for men who trust in Him (v. 19)
8. Showed me His marvelous kindness (v. 21)

Twelve things God is to His people (2 Sam 22)
1. Rock (v. 2; Ps 18:2)
2. Fortress (same ref)
3. Deliverer (same ref)

4. God of my Rock (same ref)
5. Shield (v. 3)
6. High tower (v. 3; Ps 18:2)
7. Horn of my salvation (v. 3; Ps 18:2)
8. Refuge (v. 3)
9. Savior (v. 3
10. Lamp (v. 29)
11. Buckler (v. 31)
12. Strength (v. 33)

GOD'S APPEARANCE (also see Glory)

From the Bible's 44 times that God appeared on earth, we know His following description:

Ezek 1:26 *And above the firmament that was over their heads was the likeness of a throne in appearance like a sapphire stone, and seated above the likeness of a throne was a likeness with the appearance of a Man.* AMP

Ezek 1:27-28 *From what had the appearance of His waist upward, I saw a lustre as it were glowing metal with the appearance of fire enclosed round about within it; and from the appearance of His waist downward, I saw as it were the appearance of fire, and there was brightness [of a halo] round about Him. 28 Like the appearance of the bow that is in the cloud on the day of rain, so was the appearance of the brightness round about. This was the appearance of the likeness of the glory of the Lord.* AMP

Gen 1:26 *God said, Let Us [Father, Son, and Holy Spirit] make mankind in Our image, after Our likeness.* AMP

Gen 32:30 *And Jacob called the name of the place Peniel [the face of God], saying, For I have seen God face to face, and my life is spared and not snatched away.* AMP

Ex 33:11 *And the Lord spoke to Moses face to face, as a man speaks to his friend.* AMP

Joshua saw God in a visible body having a sword in His hand (Josh 5:13-15).

God is described having:

1. Ears (2 Sam 22:7; Ps 18:6)
2. Nostrils (2 Sam 22:9; Ps 18:8, 15)
3. Mouth (2 Sam 22:9; Ps 18:8)
4. Feet (2 Sam 22:10; Ps 18:9; Ezek 1:27)
5. Body (2 Sam 22:11)
6. Form (*seen,* 2 Sam 22:11)
7. Voice (2 Sam 22:14; Ps 18:13)
8. Breath (2 Sam 22:16; Ps 18:15)
9. Arms (2 Sam 22:17)
10. Back parts (Ex 33:23)
11. Lips and tongue (Isa 30:27)
12. Eyes (Ps 11:4; 33:18)
13. Loins (Ezek 8:1-4; 1:26-28)
14. Heart (Gen 6:6; 8:21)
15. Hands and fingers (Heb 1:10; Ezek 8:3)
16. Hair, head, face (Rev 5:1-7; Dan 7:9-14; 10:5-19)

God's body appears like that of a man's. Of course, we know we are created in His image. Take that literally—His "form" is similar to the human body—at least from the loins upward—the lower part appears as the brightness of His glory. His body is not of flesh and bones, but a spirit body. Our spirit body will (and does) look like our physical body.

2 Chron 2:6 *heaven and the heaven of heavens cannot contain Him…* NKJV. Does not refer to His size, for God cannot be limited to the place heaven.

TRINITY

Acts 10:38 God anointed Jesus of Nazareth with the Holy Spirit and with power. NKJV

2 Cor 13:14 *The grace of the Lord Jesus Christ, and the love of God, and the communion of the Holy Spirit be with you all. Amen.* NKJV

1 John 5:7 *For there are three that bear witness in heaven: the Father, the Word, and the Holy Spirit.* NKJV

1 Cor 8:6 *…yet for us there is but one God, the Father, from whom are all things*

and we exist for Him; and one Lord, Jesus Christ...

Three persons cannot be one person in number---but the three can be one in perfect unity.

The Father is called God (1 Cor 8:6)
The Son is called God (Isa 9:6-7; Heb 1:8)
The Holy Spirit is called God (Acts 5:3-4)

Each is called God individually but are One in unity.
The word God is used either as singular or plural, like "sheep"

Plural pronouns are used of God
Gen 1:26 *Then God said, "Let Us make man in Our image, according to Our likeness...*

Gen 3:22 *Then the Lord God said, "Behold, the man has become like one of Us...*

John 14:23-24 *Jesus answered and said to him, "If anyone loves Me, he will keep My word; and My Father will love him, and We will come to him and make Our abode with him.*

John 17:11-12 *...that they may be one even as We are.*

The Father, the Son, and the Holy Spirit are mentioned separately in dozens of scriptures, verifying three persons make up the totality of God, One person.

John 1:14 *And the Word became flesh, and dwelt among us, and we saw His glory, glory as of the only begotten from the Father,*

John 5:30 *I do not seek My own will, but the will of Him who sent Me.*

2 John 3 *Grace, mercy and peace will be with us, from God the Father and from Jesus Christ, the Son of the Father...*

John 14:16-17 *I will ask the Father, and He will give you another Helper, that He may be with you forever; 17 that is the Spirit of truth...*

John 16:7 *...if I do not go away, the Helper will not come to you...*

Col 2:9 *...or in Him all the fullness of Deity dwells in bodily form...*

Jesus said He was not the Father over 80 times (several times just in John 14:1-12).
Jesus called God "My Father" 57 times.
The Holy Spirit is "another" from the Father and the Son in John 5:32 and 16:7-15

Two or three persons of the Godhead are referred to in every New Testament book.

GOD IS IN EVERY BELIEVER

HIS FULLNESS IS IN YOU

Phil 2:13 ...*for it is God who is at work in you, both to will and to work for His good pleasure.*

1 John 4:4-5 ...*greater is He who is in you than he who is in the world.*

John 1:16 *For of His fullness we have all received...*

1 Cor 6:19 *Or do you not know that your body is a temple of the Holy Spirit who is in you, whom you have from God...*

Eph 3:19 ...*that you may be filled up to all the fullness of God.*

Eph 2:22 ...*in whom you also are being built together into a dwelling of God in the Spirit.*

John 14:23-24 *Jesus answered and said to him, "If anyone loves Me, he will keep My word; and My Father will love him, and We will come to him and make Our abode with him.*

1 John 4:16 ...*the one who abides in love abides in God, and God abides in him.*

John 6:56-57 *He who eats My flesh and drinks My blood abides in Me, and I in him.*

HIS NATURE IS IN YOU

2 Peter 1:4 ...*by them you may become partakers of the divine nature...*

John 10:10 *I came that they may have life, and have it abundantly.*

John 10:28 ...*and I give eternal life to them, and they will never perish; and no one will snatch them out of My hand.*

John 1:3-4 ...*being that has come into being. 4 In Him was life, and the life was the Light of men.*

Eph 5:30 *...because we are members of His body.*

John 3:6-7 *...that which is born of the Spirit is spirit.*

HIS ABILITY IS IN YOU
Acts 1:8 *... but you will receive power when the Holy Spirit has come upon you*

2 Cor 3:4-6 *...toward God. 5 Not that we are adequate in ourselves to consider anything as coming from ourselves, but our adequacy is from God, 6 who also made us adequate as servants of a new covenant*

Matt 17:20 *...if you have faith the size of a mustard seed, you will say to this mountain, 'Move from here to there,' and it will move; and nothing will be impossible to you.*

John 14:12 *I say to you, he who believes in Me, the works that I do, he will do also; and greater works than these he will do...*

GRIEF

(Thoughts used from Dr. Raymond T. Brock, Tulsa, OK)

VOCABULARY OF LOSS

1. *Bereavement* is an umbrella word under which such words as grief, sorrow, mourning, and yearning are included.

2. *Grieving* is the process of expressing grief. It involves weeping, crying, and wailing in response to the death of a loved one.

3. *Grief* is an emotional attitude, a complex of emotions, used to express deep mental suffering; the strongest word to describe loss.

4. *Mourning* applies to a period of grief that follows loss by death.

5. *Sorrow* incorporates emotions used to express a major disappointment in life.

6. *Misery* is used to describe acute pain from a loss; enough to crush the human spirit.

7. *Yearning* refers to deep longing, especially when accompanied by sadness; lasts up to six months.

STEPS IN WORKING THROUGH GRIEF PROCESS

1. Shock and denial are immediate.
2. Emotional release is normal as the magnitude of the loss is acknowledged.
3. Depression comes as the reality of the loss is absorbed. Fluctuating mood cycles.
4. Psychosomatic symptoms will be experienced which include angry withdrawal, intense loneliness, and obsession over the lost person.
5. Panic sets in as focus on the loss becomes intent. The survivor must realize this in normal. He/she must begin to confront the panic and move on toward recovery.
6. Guilt emerges naturally if the survivor feels responsible for the loss. This is the hardest stage to work through.
7. Hostility with its accompanying anger and frustration frequently follows the guild.
8. Resistance to returning to business as usual, will come. Getting back to the mainstream of life is too painful to hurry. The process in greatly influenced by the quality of family support.

9. Hope emerges as the grieving person returns to normal. This is enhanced by friends over a period of months.
10. Recovery marks the time the bereaved person is again oriented to time, place, and person. He/she is ready to reenter life.

GROWTH

A STUDY

THE NATURE OF GOD DEMANDS GROWTH

Gen 1:28 *God blessed them; and God said to them, "Be fruitful and multiply, and fill the earth.*

Gen 9:1 *And God blessed Noah and his sons and said to them, "Be fruitful and multiply, and fill the earth.*

Gen 16:10-11...*the angel of the Lord said to her, "I will greatly multiply your descendants so that they will be too many to count."*

Gen 22:17-18 ...*indeed I will greatly bless you, and I will greatly multiply your seed as the stars of the heavens and as the sand which is on the seashore; and your seed shall possess the gate of their enemies.*

Lev 26:9 *So I will turn toward you and make you fruitful and multiply you...*

Jer 30:19 *From them will proceed thanksgiving And the voice of those who celebrate; And I will multiply them and they will not be diminished; I will also honor them and they will not be insignificant.*

Jer 33:22 *As the host of heaven cannot be counted and the sand of the sea cannot be measured, so I will multiply the descendants of David.*

Ezek 16:7 *I made you numerous like plants of the field.*

Ezek 37:26 *I will make a covenant of peace with them; it will be an everlasting covenant with them. And I will place them and multiply them.*

2 Cor 9:10 *Now He who supplies seed to the sower and bread for food will supply and multiply your seed for sowing and increase the harvest of your righteousness.*

Heb 6:14-15 *"I WILL SURELY BLESS YOU AND I WILL SURELY MULTIPLY YOU."*

GROWING DEEPER IN GOD

2 Cor 3:18 *But...we are being transformed into the same image... by the Spirit of the Lord.* NKJV

Rom 1:17 *...from faith to faith...* NKJV

Ps 84:7 *They go from strength to strength;* NKJV

GOD'S WORD PROMISES GROWTH
Ezek 36:37 *I will increase their men like a flock.* NKJV

Ezek 36:37 *...so shall the ruined cities be filled with flocks of men.* NKJV

2 Cor 9:10-11 *He who supplies seed to the sower, and bread for food, supply and multiply the seed you have sown and increase the fruits of your righteousness, 11 while you are enriched in everything for all liberality...* NKJV

Mark 4:14 *The sower sows the word.* NKJV

Deut 7:13 *He will love you and bless you and multiply you; He will also bless the fruit of your womb and the fruit of your land, your grain and your new wine and your oil, the increase of your cattle and the offspring of your flock...* NKJV

1 Cor 3:6-7 *God gave the increase.* NKJV

Ps 85:12 *Indeed, the Lord will give what is good, And our land will yield its produce.*

Gen 9:27 *May God enlarge Japheth, And let him dwell in the tents of Shem;*

Ex 34:24 *For I will drive out nations before you and enlarge your borders.*

Deut 12:20 *When the Lord your God extends your border as He has promised you.*

PRAISE GOD FOR GROWTH
Job 8:7 *Though your beginning was insignificant, Yet your end will increase greatly.*

Ps 71:21 *May You increase my greatness.*

Ps 115:14 *May the Lord give you increase, You and your children.*

Heb 11:1 *Now faith is the assurance of things hoped for...*

Rom 4:17 *God, who gives life to the dead and calls those things which do not exist as though they did;* NKJV

Isa 54:2-3 *Enlarge the place of your tent, And let them stretch out the curtains of your dwellings; Do not spare; Lengthen your cords, And strengthen your stakes. 3 For you shall expand to the right and to the left,* NKJV

1 Sam 2:1 *My mouth speaks boldly against my enemies, Because I rejoice in Your salvation.*

Ps 67:5-6 *Let the peoples praise You, O God; Let all the peoples praise You. 6 Then the earth shall yield her increase;* NKJV

Ps 106:47 *To give thanks to Your holy name, To triumph in Your praise.* NKJV

GROW FROM BEING FED BY THE WORD OF GOD

Mal 4:2-3 *But to you who fear My name The Sun of Righteousness shall arise With healing in His wings; And you shall go out And grow fat like stall-fed calves. 3 You shall trample the wicked, For they shall be ashes under the soles of your feet On the day that I do this...* NKJV

Prov 1:5 *A wise man will hear and increase learning...* NKJV

Acts 12:24 *But the word of God grew and multiplied.* NKJV

Acts 20:32 *So now, brethren, I commend you to God and to the word of His grace, which is able to build you up.* NKJV

1 Peter 2:2 *...as newborn babes, desire the pure milk of the word, that you may grow thereby...* NKJV

Lev 26:3-4 *If you walk in My statutes and keep My commandments, and perform them, 4 then I will give you rain in its season, the land shall yield its produce, and the trees of the field shall yield their fruit.* NKJV

GROWTH TAKES PLACE WITH ACTIVITY

Prov 14:4 *Where no oxen are, the trough is clean; But much increase comes by the strength of an ox.* NKJV

James 2:20 *...faith without works is useless*

2 Cor 9:10-11 *Now He who supplies seed to the sower and bread for food will supply and multiply your seed for sowing and increase the harvest of your righteousness; 11 you will be enriched in everything for all liberality, which through us is producing thanksgiving to God.*

GROWTH TAKES PLACE EVEN IN RUGGED SURROUNDINGS

Isa 53:2 *For He grew up before Him like a tender shoot, And like a root out of parched ground;*

Hos 14:5-6 *I will be like the dew to Israel; He will blossom like the lily, And he will take root like the cedars of Lebanon. 6 His shoots will sprout, And his beauty will be like the olive tree And his fragrance like the cedars of Lebanon.*

GROWTH TAKES PLACE IN THE ATMOSPHERE OF LOVE

Eph 4:15-16 *...but speaking the truth in love, we are to grow up in all aspects into Him who is the head, even Christ...*

Eph 4:16 *...causes the growth of the body for the building up of itself in love.*

1 Thess 3:12 *...and may the Lord cause you to increase and abound in love for one another...*

2 Thess 1:3 *We ought always to give thanks to God for you, brethren, as is only fitting, because your faith is greatly enlarged, and the love of each one of you toward one another grows ever greater;*

GROWTH BRINGS US INTO MATURE SONS

Eph 2:21-22 *...in whom the whole building, being fitted together, is growing into a holy temple in the Lord, 22 in whom you also are being built together into a dwelling of God in the Spirit.*

Eph 4:13 *...until we all attain to the unity of the faith, and of the knowledge of the Son of God, to a mature man, to the measure of the stature which belongs to the fullness of Christ.*

Eph 4:15-16 *...but speaking the truth in love, we are to grow up in all aspects into Him who is the head, even Christ, 16 from whom the whole body, being fitted and held together by what every joint supplies...*

Luke 6:40 *A pupil is not above his teacher; but everyone, after he has been fully trained, will be like his teacher.*

Rom 8:29 *For those whom He foreknew, He also predestined to become conformed to the image of His Son...*

2 Cor 3:18 *But we all, with unveiled face, beholding as in a mirror the glory of the Lord, are being transformed into the same image from glory to glory, just as from the Lord, the Spirit.*

Gal 4:19-20 *My children, with whom I am again in labor until Christ is formed in you...*

GUIDANCE
A STUDY

THE HOLY SPIRIT WILL GUIDE

John 16:13-14 *But when He, the Spirit of truth, comes, He will guide you into all the truth; for He will not speak on His own initiative, but whatever He hears, He will speak; and He will disclose to you what is to come.*

Rom 8:14-15 *For all who are being led by the Spirit of God, these are sons of God.*

Ps 73:24 *You will guide me with Your counsel.* AMP

HIS EYES WILL GUIDE

Ps 32:8 *I will instruct you and teach you in the way which you should go; I will counsel you with My eye upon you.*

Prov 23:26 *My son, give me your heart, And let your eyes observe my ways.* NKJV

2 Chron 16:9 *For the eyes of the Lord run to and fro throughout the whole earth, to show Himself strong on behalf of those whose heart is loyal to Him.* NKJV

Prov 15:3 *The eyes of the Lord are in every place, Keeping watch on the evil and the good.* NKJV

Prov 3:6 *In all your ways acknowledge Him, And He shall direct your paths.* NKJV

HIS WORD WILL GUIDE

Ps 73:24 *With Your counsel You will guide me...*

2 Tim 2:7 *Consider what I say, for the Lord will give you understanding in everything.*

Ps 25:14 *The secret of the Lord is for those who fear Him, And He will make them know His covenant.*

Ps 119:133 *Establish my footsteps in Your word...*

2 Sam 22:31 *As for God, His way is perfect; the word of the Lord is true.* AMP

Ps 27:11 *Teach me Your way, O Lord, And lead me in a level path Because of my foes.*

Prov 4:18 *But the path of the righteous is like the light of dawn, That shines brighter and brighter until the full day.*

Ps 16:11 *You will make known to me the path of life; In Your presence is fullness of joy; In Your right hand there are pleasures forever.*

Prov 3:6 *In all your ways acknowledge Him, And He will make your paths straight.*

Prov 15:19 *The way of the sluggard is overgrown with thorns [it pricks, lacerates, and entangles him], but the way of the righteous is plain and raised like a highway.* AMP

Prov 15:24 *The path of the wise leads upward to life...* AMP

2 Sam 22:33 *God is my strong Fortress; He guides the blameless in His way and sets him free.* AMP

Ps 5:8 *Lead me, O Lord, in Your righteousness because of my enemies; make Your way level (straight and right) before my face.* AMP

Prov 3:5-6 *Lean on, trust in, and be confident in the Lord with all your heart and mind and do not rely on your own insight or understanding. 6 In all your ways know, recognize, and acknowledge Him, and He will direct and make straight and plain your paths.* AMP

Prov 3:17 *Her ways are highways of pleasantness, and all her paths are peace.* AMP

Isa 30:21 *"And your ears shall hear a word behind you saying This is the way, walk in it, when you tum to the right hand, and when you turn to the left."* AMP

HE GUIDES US SAFELY

Ps 78:53 *And He led them on safely and in confident trust, so that they feared not.* AMP

Ps 23:2 *He makes me lie down in [fresh, tender] green pastures; He leads me beside the still and restful waters.* AMP

Ps 91:11 *For He will give His angels [especial] charge over you to accompany and defend and preserve you in all your ways.* AMP

Prov 3:23 *Then you will walk in your way securely and in confident trust, and you shall not dash your foot or stumble.* AMP

INTEGRITY WILL GUIDE
Prov 11:3 *The integrity of the upright will guide them...*

PEACE WILL GUIDE
Rom 14:19-20 *So then we pursue the things which make for peace and the building up of one another.*

GOOD WILL GUIDE
Ps 38:20 *I follow the thing that is good.* AMP

HE GUIDES IN DAILY NEEDS
Isa 58:11 *And the Lord shall guide you continually.* AMP

Deut 29:5 *I have led you forty years in the wilderness...* AMP

Isa 48:21 *And they thirsted not when He led them through the deserts; He caused the waters to flow out of the rock for them; He split the rock also, and the waters gushed out.* AMP

HABITS

Ps 23:1 *The Lord is my shepherd; I shall not want.* NKJV

1 Cor 10:13 *No temptation has overtaken you except such as is common to man; but God is faithful, who will not allow you to be tempted beyond what you are able, but with the temptation will also make the way of escape, that you may be able to bear it.* NKJV

Phil 4:5 *Let all men know and perceive and recognize your unselfishness (your considerateness, your forbearing spirit).* AMP

Isa 41:10 *Fear not [there is nothing to fear], for I am with you; do not look around you in terror and be dismayed, for I am your God. I will strengthen and harden you to difficulties, yes, I will help you; yes, I will hold you up and retain you with My [victorious] right hand of rightness and justice.* AMP

2 Tim 1:7 *For God has not given us a spirit of fear, but of power and of love and of a sound mind.* NKJV

Gal 5:1 *Stand fast therefore in the liberty by which Christ has made us free, and do not be entangled again with a yoke of bondage.* NKJV

Gal 5:16-17 *...you shall not fulfill the lust of the flesh.* NKJV

Rom 8:5-6 *For those who live according to the flesh set their minds on the things of the flesh, but those who live according to the Spirit, the things of the Spirit. 6 For to be carnally minded is death, but to be spiritually minded is life and peace.* NKJV

Rom 8:13 *...if you live according to the flesh you will die;* NKJV

Gal 5:24 *And those who are Christ's have crucified the flesh with its passions and desires.* NKJV

2 Cor 5:17-18 *Therefore, if anyone is in Christ, he is a new creation; old things have passed away; behold, all things have become new.* NKJV

Phil 4:13 *I can do all things through Christ who strengthens me.* NKJV

2 Cor 3:17 *Now the Lord is the Spirit; and where the Spirit of the Lord is, there is liberty.* NKJV

Matt 11:28-29 *Come to Me, all you who labor and are heavy laden, and I will give you rest.* NKJV   skh

HAPPY (also see JOY)

Ps 1:1 *BLESSED (HAPPY, fortunate, prosperous, and enviable) is the man who walks and lives...* AMP

Ps 32:1 *BLESSED (HAPPY, fortunate, to be envied) is he who has forgiveness of his transgression continually exercised upon him, whose sin is covered.* AMP

Ps 41:1 *BLESSED (HAPPY, fortunate, to be envied) is he who considers the weak and the poor; the Lord will deliver him in the time of evil and trouble.* AMP

Ps 84:12 *O Lord of hosts, blessed (happy, fortunate, to be envied) is the man who trusts in You.* AMP

Ps 112:1 *PRAISE THE Lord! (Hallelujah!) Blessed (happy, fortunate, to be envied) is the man who fears (reveres and worships) the Lord, who delights greatly in His commandments.* AMP

Matt 5:3- *Blessed (happy, to be envied, and spiritually prosperous — with life-joy and satisfaction in God's favor and salvation, regardless of their outward conditions) are the poor in spirit (the humble, who rate themselves insignificant), for theirs is the kingdom of heaven!* AMP

John 20:29 *Blessed and happy and to be envied are those who have never seen Me and yet have believed and adhered to and trusted and relied on Me.* AMP

ℋEALING

A STUDY

Luke 10:9 *And heal the sick...* NKJV

Ex 23:25 *I will take sickness away from the midst of you.* NKJV

James 5:14 *Is anyone among you sick? He should call in the church elders (the spiritual guides). And they should pray over him, anointing him with oil in the Lord's name.* AMP

Ex 15:26 *...and said, "If you diligently heed the voice of the Lord your God and do what is right in His sight, give ear to His commandments and keep all His statutes, I will put none of the diseases on you which I have brought on the Egyptians. For I am the Lord who heals you."* NKJV

Prov 4:20-22 *...my son, give attention to my words; Incline your ear to my sayings. 21 Do not let them depart from your eyes; Keep them in the midst of your heart; 22 For they are life to those who find them, And health to all their flesh.* NKJV

Isa 58:8 *Your healing shall spring forth speedily...* NKJV

Prov 3:7-8 *Do not be wise in your own eyes; Fear the Lord and depart from evil. 8 It will be health to your flesh, And strength to your bones.* NKJV

3 John 2 *Beloved, I pray that you may prosper in all things and be in health, just as your soul prospers.* NKJV

Prov 12:18 *...the tongue of the wise promotes health.* NKJV

Prov 16:24 *Pleasant words are like a honeycomb, Sweetness to the soul and health to the bones.* NKJV

2 Kings 20:5 *"Return and tell Hezekiah the leader of My people, 'Thus says the Lord, the God of David your father: "I have heard your prayer, I have seen your tears; surely I will heal you."'"* NKJV

2 Chron 16:12 *And in the thirty-ninth year of his reign, Asa became diseased in his feet, and his malady was severe; yet in his disease he did not seek the Lord, but the physicians.*NKJV

Num 12:13 *So Moses cried out to the Lord, saying, "Please heal her, O God, I pray!"* NKJV

Ps 30:2 *O Lord my God, I cried out to You, And You healed me.* NKJV

Mark 10:46-52 *...blind Bartimaeus, the son of Timaeus, sat by the road begging. 47 And when he heard that it was Jesus of Nazareth, he began to cry out and say, "Jesus, Son of David, have mercy on me!" 51 So Jesus answered and said to him, "What do you want Me to do for you?" The blind man said to Him, "Rabboni, that I may receive my sight." 52 Then Jesus said to him, "Go your way; your faith has made you well." And immediately he received his sight and followed Jesus on the road.* NKJV

Mark 2:10-12 *He said to the paralytic, 11 "I say to you, arise, take up your bed, and go to your house." 12 Immediately he arose, took up the bed, and went out in the presence of them all.* NKJV

Mark 10:52 *Then Jesus said to him, "Go your way; your faith has made you well." And immediately he received his sight and followed Jesus on the road.* NKJV

Acts 3:6-8 *"Silver and gold I do not have, but what I do have I give you: In the name of Jesus Christ of Nazareth, rise up and walk." 7 And he took him by the right hand and lifted him up, and immediately his feet and ankle bones received strength. 8 So he, leaping up, stood and walked.* NKJV

Acts 9:34 *And Peter said to him, "Aeneas, Jesus the Christ heals you. Arise and make your bed." Then he arose immediately.* NKJV

Acts 14:9-11 *...he had faith to be healed, 10 said with a loud voice, "Stand up straight on your feet!" And he leaped and walked.* NKJV

Mal 4:2-3 *But for you who fear My name, the sun of righteousness will rise with healing in its wings; and you will go forth and skip about like calves from the stall.*

Ps 105:37 *...and there was not one feeble person among their tribes.* AMP

Jer 33:5-6 *Behold, I will bring to it health and healing, and I will heal them; and I will reveal to them an abundance of peace and truth.*

1 Peter 2:24 *...and He Himself bore our sins in His body on the cross, so that we might die to sin and live to righteousness; for by His wounds you were healed.*

Ps 103:3 *Who heals all your diseases;*

Hos 6:1 *COME AND let us return to the Lord, for He has torn so that He may heal us; He has stricken so that He may bind us up.* AMP

Jer 30:17 *For I will restore health to you, and I will heal your wounds, says the Lord...* AMP

Isa 58:11 *And the Lord shall guide you continually and satisfy you in drought and in dry places and make strong your bones. And you shall be like a watered garden and like a spring of water whose waters fail not.* AMP

Matt 12:15 *Many followed Him, and He healed them all.*

Acts 5:16 *...the people from the cities in the vicinity of Jerusalem were coming together, bringing people who were sick or afflicted with unclean spirits, and they were all being healed.*

1 Peter 1:23 *...having been born again, not of corruptible seed but incorruptible,* NKJV

Rom 10:17 *So then faith comes by hearing, and hearing by the word of God.* NKJV

Matt 18:18-19 *"Assuredly, I say to you, whatever you bind on earth will be bound in heaven, and whatever you loose on earth will be loosed in heaven. 19 "Again I say to you that if two of you agree on earth concerning anything that they ask, it will be done for them by My Father in heaven."* NKJV

Mark 16:18 *...they will lay hands on the sick, and they will recover.* NKJV

James 1:16-17 *Every good gift and every perfect gift is from above, and comes down from the Father of lights.* NKJV

Ps 107:20 *He sent His word and healed them...* NKJV

- Isa 53:5 *And by His stripes we are healed.* NKJV (written about 750 BCE)

- 1 Peter 2:24-25 *...by whose stripes you were healed.* NKJV (written about 815 years later in 65 CE)

- Matt 8:18 *...that it might be fulfilled which was spoken by Isaiah the prophet, saying: "He Himself took our infirmities And bore our sicknesses."* NKJV

The New Testament is established on better promises than the Old Testament (Heb 8:6).

FOURTEEN HEBREW (Old Testament) AND GREEK (New Testament) WORDS IN THE BIBLE THAT REFER TO PHYSICAL HEALING

1. "rapha"

Translated *cure* in Jer 33:6

Translated *made whole* in Job 5:1
Translated *heal* in Dt 32:39

Translated *healed* in Gen 20:17
Translated *heals* in Ex 15:26
Translated *thoroughly healed* in Ex 21:19
Translated *physician* in Gen 50:2

2. "marpay"

Translated *healing* in Ier 14:19
Translated *health* in Pro 4:22
Translated *cure* in Jer 33:6
Translated *remedy* in 2 Chr 26:16
Translated *sound* in health in Pro 14:30
Translated *wholesome* in Pro 15:4

3. "yeshuwah"

Translated *health* in Ps 42:11

Translated *deliverance* in Ps 44:4

Translated *salvation* in Ps 91:16 (the entire 91st Psalm teaches perfect healing and health physically, so the salvation of v. 16 includes the body as well as soul).

4. "arubah"

Means *restoration to sound health* (Jer 8:22)

5. "chabash"

Means *healer* (Isa 3:6) and to *bind up* or *heal* in Isa 30:26 and Ezek 34:16)

6. "rifooth"

Means *health* (Prov 3:8)

7. "therapeuo"

Translated *heal* in Matt 8:7

Translated *healed* in Matt 4:23-24

Translated *cure* in Matt 17:16

Translated *cured* in Luke 7:21

8. "iama"

Means *healing* or *repair* in 1 Cor 12:9, 28, 30

9. "iaomai"

Translated *heal* in Matt 13:15

Translated *healed* in Matt 8:8

Translated *healing* in Acts 10:38

Translated *whole* in Matt 15:28

10. "iasis"

Meaning *healing* and *cure* in Luke 23:32; Acts 4:22

11. "fugiano"

Meaning *sound health* (3 John 2)

12. "hugies"

Meaning *healthy, sound and whole* in Matt 12:13; Mark 3:5; Luke 5:31

13. "sodzo"

Meaning to *save, deliver, protect, and heal* in Matt 9:21; Mark 5:29; Acts 4:9; Luke 8:36

14. "dia-sodzo"

Meaning to *heal thoroughly, make perfectly whole* in Matt 14:35; Luke 7:3

CONSIDER

Isa 53:3-5

3 He is despised and rejected by men,
A <u>Man of sorrows</u> and acquainted with <u>grief</u>.
And we hid, as it were, our faces from Him;
He was despised, and we did not esteem Him.
4 Surely He has <u>borne</u> our griefs
And <u>carried</u> our sorrows;
Yet we esteemed Him <u>stricken</u>,
Smitten by God, and afflicted.
5 But He was <u>wounded</u> for our transgressions,
He was <u>bruised</u> for our iniquities;
The chastisement for our peace was upon Him,
And by His stripes we are healed. NKJV

"Man of sorrows" He was a man of sorrows because He carried our sorrows. He personally had no sin, sickness, pain or suffering on account of His own self and sins; but we have these in abundance, and since He came into the world to carry them for us He had to become identified with us in our sufferings by taking them upon Himself and bearing them unto death so that we might be free from them. Therefore, sorrow became a characteristic of His life during His sufferings. He no doubt had sorrows from the time His sensitive, pure, sinless, and untainted life began to contact the sins, depravities, corruptions, sicknesses, diseases, and pains of others.

"Grief/griefs" The Hebrew word *choliy* and means sickness. The words translated" grief" and" griefs" in v 3-4 should be translated sickness and sicknesses as recognized by most other translators (such as Berkeley, Septuagint and Moffatt)

"Borne" The Hebrew word *nasa* meaning to lift, bear, carry away, erase, take away. The idea is that of one person taking the burden of another and placing it on himself, as the flood lifted up the ark (Ps 103:12; Matt 8:16-17). Christ bore are sicknesses, then they were taken away!

"Carried" The Hebrew word *cabal* meaning bear, burden (Gen 49:15; 2 Chron 2:2; Eccl12:5). The idea is the full load is borne by the one carrying it so that all others might be free of it. Christ bore all our sicknesses and pains, so that we do not need to carry them.

"Stricken" The Hebrew word *naga* meaning strike violently, bring down, mite, touch in Deut. 21:4

"Wound" The Hebrew word *chalal* meaning to bore, slay, pierce---eferring to piercing the hands, feet, and side, in Isa 51:9; Ps 109:22.

"Bruise" The Hebrew word *daka* to crumble, beat to pieces, break, crush, smite—referring to the stripes, cuts and bodily sufferings. It was by this particular phase of punishment that bodily healing was provided for all.

WHAT TO DO AFTER HANDS ARE LAID ON YOU

1. You've acted on Jesus' words: "And these signs shall follow them that believe ... they shall lay hands on the sick, and they shall recover" (Mark 16:17-18). You. as a believer, may have laid your own hands upon yourself for healing, or another believer may have laid hands upon you for your healing. In either case. you can have great assurance that there will be a performance of what Jesus has promised, for He watches over His Word to do it. This is a very positive promise: you will recover. Jesus did not say, "You might recover," or "I hope that you will recover," or "Recovery is possible." No! Without reservation, Jesus declared, "You will recover!" Praise the Lord that you are now recovering!

2. If you have not received an instantaneous miracle, do not cast away your confidence. When Jesus walked this earth, He healed people in various ways—many were healed instantly, others were healed gradually. Whether you are healed instantly, or a gradual mending process has begun, you can go your way praising Him with confidence that He is keeping His Word with you.

3. Begin to declare your healing. "I am recovering. Jesus said so and I believe His Word. I am not going on how I look, how I feel, or how others think I look. I have accepted Jesus' Word at face value: I am recovering."

4. James, chapter one, declares that when you ask God for anything, you must ask in faith, never doubting. *But he must ask in faith without any doubting, for the one who doubts is like the surf of the sea, driven and tossed by the wind. For that man ought not to expect that he will receive anything from the Lord* (NASU),

Anything includes healing. Your role in this drama of faith is to possess unwavering confidence that the Lord will keep His Word. If you waver in your faith, then you deny yourself the Lord's healing. Do not waver in your declaration of faith. Say and believe "By his stripes I am healed."

5. Until your healing is fully manifested, you' will be engaged in a fight of faith. It is not a fight against God or His Word, but a fight against the thief who

came to "kill, steal and destroy" (John 10: 10). In this conflict, use the weapons of your warfare which are mighty through God to the pulling down of satanic strongholds. Confess boldly, unwaveringly, "By His stripes I am healed!"

6. Act like you are recovering. Begin to do things you could not do before. Praise the Lord that you are recovering. When others enquire about your condition, simply share with them the fact that you are recovering, (because Jesus said so).

7. The devil doesn't want you to recover. Here's how to deal with him: "Satan, I resist you in the name of Jesus, for it is written, 'they shall lay hands on the sick and they shall recover.' In Jesus' mighty name, I am recovering!"

8. God is no respecter of persons. Thousands of people have been healed through the ministry of laying on of hands. What God has done for others He is doing for you! Praise Him now for your recovery!

*H*EAVEN

A STUDY

The heavens were created by God, exactly like He created the earth and beings. He spoke the materials into existence and then formed the materials into being.

> 2 Peter 3:5. 7 *For this they willfully forget: that by the word of God the heavens were of old, and the earth standing out of water and in the water…7 But the heavens and the earth which are now preserved by the same word…* NKJV

THREE HEAVENS
1.Clouds

Ps 104:2 *Who stretch out the heavens like a curtain. He lays the beams of His upper chambers in the waters, Who makes the clouds His chariot, Who walks on the wings of the wind.* NKJV

Job 26:8 *He wraps up the waters in His clouds*

Ps 77:17-18 *The clouds poured out water; The skies gave forth a sound; Your arrows flashed here and there. 18 The sound of Your thunder was in the whirlwind; The lightnings lit up the world;*

Dan 7:13 *"I was watching in the night visions, And behold, One like the Son of Man, Coming with the clouds of Heaven.* NKJV

2.Starry Space

Gen 1:14-15 *Then God said, "Let there be lights in the expanse of the heavens to separate the day from the night, and let them be for signs and for seasons and for days and years; 15 and let them be for lights in the expanse of the heavens to give light on the earth"*

Gen 15:5 *And He took him outside and said, "Now look toward the heavens, and count the stars.*

Gen 22:17 *I will greatly bless you, and I will greatly multiply your seed as the stars of the heavens*

Deut 1:10-11 *The Lord your God has multiplied you, and behold, you are this day like the stars of heaven in number.*

3.Planet Heaven

2 Cor 12:2 *...a man was caught up to the third heaven.*

Isa 14:13 *...you said in your heart, 'I will ascend to heaven; I will raise my throne above the stars of God...'*

Isa 66:1 *Thus says the Lord, "Heaven is My throne and the earth is My footstool..."*

Rev 21:1 *And I saw the holy city, new Jerusalem, coming down out of heaven from God.*

Rev 21:10 *...the holy city, Jerusalem, coming down out of heaven from God.*

Gen 1:1-2 *In the beginning God created the heavens and the earth.*

FACTS CONCERNING HEAVEN

The words Heaven and Heavens are used 718 times in Scripture. They mean the air, clouds, sky, expanse, stars, and the planet on which Cod dwells.

Created by God

Gen 1:1 *IN THE beginning God (prepared, formed, fashioned, and) created the heavens and the earth.* AMP

Gen 2:2 *And on the seventh day God ended His work which He had done; and He rested on the seventh day from all His work which He had done.* AMP

Ps 8:3 *When I view and consider Your heavens, the work of Your fingers, the moon and the stars, which You have ordained and established...* AMP

Created before the earth

Gen 1:1-2 *In the beginning God created the heavens and the earth. 2 The earth was without form, and void; and darkness was on the face of the deep.* NKJV

Job 38:4 *Where were you when I laid the foundations of the earth?* NKJV

Located in the Northern part of universe

Isa 14:12-13 *"How you are fallen from heaven, O Lucifer, son of the morning! How you are cut down to the ground, you who weakened the nations! 13 For you have said in your heart: 'I will ascend into heaven, I will exalt my throne above the stars of God; I will also sit on the mount of the congregation On the farthest sides of the north'";* NKJV

Ps 75:6 *For exaltation comes neither from the east Nor from the west nor from the south.* NKJV

Located in the highest part of creation

Job 22:12 *Is not God in the height of heaven? And see the highest stars, how lofty they are!* NKJV

Eph 1:21 *...far above all principality and power and might and dominion.* NKJV

Eph 4:10 *He who descended is also the One who ascended far above all the heavens.*
NKJV

Round like the earth

Job 22:14 *And He walks above the circle of heaven.* NKJV

Ps 19:6 *Its rising is from one end of heaven, And its circuit to the other end;* NKJV

Isa 40:22 *It is He who sits above the circle of the earth.* NKJV

Size

Unknown; however, from the size of its cities (Rev 21: 9-27) and from number of inhabitants (Heb 12:22-23; Jer 33:22) it is probably larger than earth.

Kingdoms in heaven

Col 1:16 *...the things we can see and the things we can't; the spirit world with its kings and kingdoms, its rulers and authorities;* TLB
Eph 3:10-11 *To show to all the rulers in heaven how perfectly wise he is when all of his family-Jews and Gentiles alike-are seen to be joined together in his Church.* TLB

1 Peter 3:22 *And now Christ is in heaven, sitting in the place of honor next to God the Father, with all the angels and powers of heaven bowing before him and obeying him.* TLB

Laws in heaven

Job 38:33 *Do you know the laws of the universe and how the heavens influence the earth?* TLB

Jer 31:35 *...the Lord,*
Who gives the sun for light by day And the fixed order of the moon and the stars for light by night.

Inhabitants in heaven

Dan 4:35 *He does according to His will in the host of heaven.*

Job 1:6 *Now there was a day when the sons of God came to present themselves before the Lord, and Satan also came among them.*

Ezek 28:15 *You were blameless in your ways From the day you were created Until unrighteousness was found in you.*

Ezek 28:16 *And you sinned; Therefore I have cast you as profane From the mountain of God.*

Rev 12:12 *For this reason, rejoice, O heavens and you who dwell in them.*

Concerning heaven:

A better country (Heb 11:10)
A paradise (2 Cor 12:1-4; Rev 2:7)
Has real cities (Heb 11:10-15; Rev 21:2; 9:27)
Mansions (John 14:1-3)
*Temples (*Ps 11:4; Rev 3:12; 7:15; Isa 6:1)
Foundations (Job 38:4-7; 2 Sam 22:8)
Golden altar (Rev 8:3-5)
Thrones (Isa 6:1-7)
Books (Lk 10:20; Heb 12:23; Rev 5:1; 13:8)
Swords, sickles (1 Chr 21:16, 27, 30; Rev 14:14, 17)
Keys, chains (Rev 9:1;20:1)
Trumpets (Rev 8:2)

Bowls (Rev 15:7)

Tables (Lk 22:30)

Food (Rev 2:7, 17; 22:1-3)

Chariots (2 Ki 2:11; 6:17; Zech 6:1-8)

Furniture (Heb 8:5; 9:23; Ex 25:40)

Floors, lamps, rainbows etc. (Rev 4:3; 5-6; 15:2)

Fountains of water (Rev 7:17)

Musical instruments (Rev 4:8-11; 14;1-5)

Clothing (Dan 7:9; 10:5; Matt 28:3; Rev 4:4)

Feasts (Lk 22:16, 30)

Drinks (Lk 22:18; Rev 7:17)

Bread (Ps 8:34-35; Jn 6:31)

Roast Lamb (Lk 22:16)

Fruits (Rev 2:7; 22:2)

Animals (2 Ki 2:11; 6:17; Rev 19:11, 14, 21)

Inhabitants (Jer 33:22; Heb 12:22-23; Rev 12:12)

Trees (Rev 2:7; 22:1-3)

Streets (Rev 2:7; 22:1-3)

Mountains (Rev 14:1; Heb12:22-23)

Eight persons/things in heaven from Heb 12:

1. The heavenly Mount Sion (v. 22; Rom 11:26; Rev 14:1)
2. The capital city of God (v. 22; 11:10, 16; 13:14; John 14)
3. Innumerable angels (v. 22; 1:5-14; Rev 5:11-14)
4. God the Judge of all (v. 23)
5. The Church of the firstborn (v. 23; Col 1:18)
6. The spirits of the just (v. 23; Rev 6:9-11)
7. Jesus (v. 24; Matt 26:28; Heb 9:15)
8. The blood of Christ (v. 24; Matt 26:28; Col 1:29)

Six things not in heaven from Rev 21 and 22

1. Sorrow (21:4)   4. Death (21:4)
2. Crying (21:4)   5. Curse (22:3)
3. Pain (21:4)   6. Night (22:5)

As awesome as the heavens are, they will all disintegrate and disappear like smoke

Isa 34:4 *All the host of heaven shall be dissolved, And the heavens shall be rolled up like a scroll*; NKJV

Isa 51:6 *Lift up your eyes to the heavens,*
And look on the earth beneath.
For the heavens will vanish away like smoke,
The earth will grow old like a garment,
And those who dwell in it will die in like manner;
But My salvation will be forever,
And My righteousness will not be abolished. NKJV

But we always have in mind the greatness of God:

Ps 57:5 *Be exalted, O God, above the heavens; Let Your glory be above all the earth.* NKJV

There are times when we need God's help! Here are scriptures which promise His help for you.

Ps 33:20 *Our soul waits for the Lord; He is our help and our shield.*

Ps 46:1-2 *God is our refuge and strength, A very present help in trouble. 2 Therefore we will not fear,*

Ps 115:11 *All of you, his people, trust in him. He is your helper; he is your shield.* TLB

Ps 124:8 *Our help is in the name of the Lord, Who made heaven and earth.*

Isa 41:10-11 *'Do not fear, for I am with you; Do not anxiously look about you, for I am your God. I will strengthen you, surely I will help you, Surely I will uphold you with My righteous right hand.' 11 "Behold, all those who are angered at you will be shamed and dishonored; Those who contend with you will be as nothing and will perish..."*

Rom 8:26 *...the Spirit also helps our weakness;*

Heb 4:16 *Therefore let us draw near with confidence to the throne of grace, so that we may receive mercy and find grace to help in time of need.*

Heb 13:6 *...we confidently say, "THE LORD IS MY HELPER, I WILL NOT BE AFRAID. WHAT WILL MAN DO TO ME?"*

Luke 18:7-8 *And will not [our just] God defend and protect and avenge His elect (His chosen ones), who cry to Him day and night? Will He defer them and delay help on their behalf? 8 I tell you, He will defend and protect and avenge them speedily.* AMP

HOLY SPIRIT

Luke 11:13 *If you then, being evil, know how to give good gifts to your children, how much more will your heavenly Father give the Holy Spirit to those who ask Him?"*

Acts 1:4 *And while being in their company and eating with them, He commanded them not to leave Jerusalem but to wait for what the Father had promised, Of which [He said] you have heard Me speak.* AMP

John 4:24 *God is a Spirit (a spiritual Being) and those who worship Him must worship Him in spirit and in truth (reality).* AMP

Rom 8:26 *So too the [Holy] Spirit comes to our aid and bears us up in our weakness; for we do not know what prayer to offer nor how to offer it worthily as we ought, but the Spirit Himself goes to meet our supplication and pleads in our behalf with unspeakable yearnings and groanings too deep for utterance.* AMP

Eph 4:30 *And do not grieve the Holy Spirit of God [do not offend or vex or sadden Him].* AMP

1 John 4:13 *He has given (imparted) to us of His [Holy] Spirit.* AMP

1 John 3:23 *He [really] lives and makes His home in us: by the [Holy] Spirit Whom He has given us.* AMP

Acts 2:3-4 *And there appeared to them tongues as of fire distributing themselves, and they rested on each one of them. 4 And they were all filled with the Holy Spirit and began to speak with other tongues, as the Spirit was giving them utterance.*

Acts 1:8 *...but you will receive power when the Holy Spirit has come upon you.*

Acts 8:14-17 *Now when the apostles in Jerusalem heard that Samaria had received the word of God, they sent them Peter and John, 15 who came down and prayed for them that they might receive the Holy Spirit. 16 For He had not yet fallen upon any of them; they had simply been baptized in the name of the Lord*

Jesus. 17 Then they began laying their hands on them, and they were receiving the Holy Spirit.

Acts 10:44 *While Peter was still speaking these words, the Holy Spirit fell upon all those who were listening to the message.*

Acts 11:16-17 *And I remembered the word of the Lord, how He used to say, 'John baptized with water, but you will be baptized with the Holy Spirit.*

Acts 19:2 *He said to them, "Did you receive the Holy Spirit when you believed?"*

Eph 1:13 *In Him, you also, after listening to the message of truth, the gospel of your salvation—having also believed, you were sealed in Him with the Holy Spirit of promise.*

Mark 11:24 *Therefore I say to you, all things for which you pray and ask, believe that you have received them, and they will be granted you.*

Matt 7:7 *Ask, and it will be given to you; seek, and you will find; knock, and it will be opened to you.*

Joel 2:28 *…It will come about after this That I will pour out My Spirit on all mankind;*

John 14:26 *But the Helper, the Holy Spirit, whom the Father will send in My name, He will teach you all things, and bring to your remembrance all that I said to you.*

John 7:39 *But this He spoke of the Spirit, whom those who believed in Him were to receive; for the Spirit was not yet given, because Jesus was not yet glorified.*

1 Cor 14:14-15 *For if I pray in a tongue, my spirit prays, but my mind is unfruitful. 15 What is the outcome then? I will pray with the spirit and I will pray with the mind also; I will sing with the spirit and I will sing with the mind also.*

John 4:24 *God is spirit, and those who worship Him must worship in spirit.*

Eph 6:18 *With all prayer and petition pray at all times in the Spirit…*

.

HOPE

Hope is the picture which the Holy Spirit paints on the canvas of our heart and hope working along with faith will come to pass. The force of faith in action by you will frame that picture and bring it into manifestation.

Heb 11:1 *NOW FAITH is the assurance (the confirmation, the title deed) of the things [we] hope for, being the proof of things [we] do not see and the conviction of their reality [faith perceiving as real fact what is not revealed to the senses].* AMP

Rom 8:24-25 *For in [this] hope we were saved. But hope [the object of] which is seen is not hope. For how can one hope for what he already sees? 25 But if we hope for what is still unseen by us, we wait for it with patience and composure.* AMP

Heb 6:19 *[Now] we have this [hope] as a sure and steadfast anchor of the soul [it cannot slip and it cannot break down under whoever steps out upon it.* AMP

Ps 119:114 *You are my hiding place and my shield; I hope in Your word.* AMP

Ps 147:11 *The Lord takes pleasure in those who reverently and worshipfully fear Him, in those who hope in His mercy and loving-kindness.* AMP

Eph 2:12 *[Remember] that you were at that time separated (living apart) from Christ... [excluded from all part in Him].* AMP

Eph 2:12 *And you had no hope (no promise); you were in the world without God.* AMP

1 Tim 6:17 *...nor to set their hopes on uncertain riches, but on God, Who richly and ceaselessly provides us with everything for [our] enjoyment.* AMP

1 Tim 1:1 *...Christ Jesus (the Messiah), our Hope...* AMP

FOUNDATION FOR BELIEF
(Gently lifted from my book: *Essence of Christian Belief*, table of contents)

1.God
     Our belief begins IN God. He is the Maker of all and allowed for the sacrifice of His Son for our sins. "For God so loved the world that He gave His Son…"

2. The Bible
3. Jesus Christ
4. The Holy Spirit
5. Man
6. The Church
7. The Future

SEVEN THINGS I KNOW AS A BELIEVER:
1. I'M SAVED
2. I HAVE SECURITY IN KNOWING I AM BORN-AGAIN
3. I AM A NEW CREATURE IN CHRIST
4. I HAVE BEEN DELIVERED
5. I AM REDEEMED
6. I AM BLESSED
7. I AM AN OVERCOMER

I BELIEVE....................
(from Pastor Stan Tharp)

- in the beginning God created the heavens and the earth *(Gen 1:1)*
- likewise, Jesus Christ is the incarnate Word of God who was in the beginning and nothing that was created came into being apart from Him. *(John 1:1-3)*
- in the triune *God…God the Father* who knows our needs, Jesus said, "even before we ask." *(Matt. 6:8)*

- in the triune God...God the Son, and the Bible says "God so loved the world that He gave His only begotten Son that whosoever believes in Him would not perish but have everlasting life. *(John 3:16)*
- in the triune God...*God the Spirit,* and the Bible says that God the *Spirit* is our Comforter, He is our Guide, He is our Convicter, He is our Baptizer, who grants us gifts. *(John 16:5-15)*
- that Jesus Christ is my Savior, that He is the Alpha and the Omega, the Beginning, and the End. *(Rev 1:8, 21:62; 2:13)*
- Jesus is the resurrection and the life (John 11:25) who gave us life more abundantly. *(John 10:10)*
- that He is the only begotten Son as begotten from the Father *(Matt 3:7; 16:16; Mark 14:26)*
- He went to prepare a place for me that where He is I may be also, and He is coming back for me. *(John 14:2)*
- He said, "I am coming quickly and my reward is in My right hand." *(Rev 2:12)*
- He is returning someday as the King of kings and the Lord of lords, and at the name of Jesus every knee shall bow and every tongue will confess Jesus Christ is Lord to the glory God the Father. *(1 Tim 6:15; Rom 14:11; Phil 2:9-11)*
- The Lord is my Shepherd and I shall not want. *(Ps 23)*
- God is intimately acquainted with all my ways, and my soul knows it very well. *(Ps 139:1-4,14)*
- He is mindful of my frame, that I am but dust, and because He is mindful of my frailties. *(Ps 139:13-15)*
- His grace is sufficient for me and His power is perfected in my weakness. *(2 Cor. 12:9)*
- I am more than a conqueror through Him who loved me, *(Rom 8:37)* and I can do all things through Jesus Christ who strengthens me. *(Phil 4:13)*
- I've learned to be content in whatever circumstances--whether of humility or circumstances of exaltation--because of Jesus Christ, *(Phil 4:11)* that even though I walk through the valley of the shadow of death I will fear no evil. *(Ps 23)*
- Jesus will never leave me nor forsake me. *(Heb 13:5)*
- The Peace of God that surpasses all comprehension shall guard my heart and mind in Christ Jesus. *(Phil 4:7)*

- I consider it all joy when I encounter various trials knowing the testing of my faith produces endurance and it has its result in me, that I might be perfect and complete, lacking in nothing. *(James 1:2-4)*
- Nothing can separate me from the love of God that is in Christ Jesus, our Lord. *(Rom 8:38-39)*
- He is the Way, the Truth and the Life. No one comes to the Father but by Him. *(John 14:6)*
- You must choose this day whom you will serve...but as for me and my house, we will serve the Lord. *(Joshua 24:15)*

I SAID:

I said, "I CAN'T GO ON"...but Jesus said "I WILL CARRY YOU."

I said, "I AM TOO TIRED"...but Jesus said "I WILL GIVE YOU REST."

I said, "THIS IS IMPOSSIBLE"...but Jesus said "ALL THINGS ARE POSSIBLE."

I said, "I AM STARVING"...but Jesus said "I AM THE BREAD OF LIFE."

I said, "I AM DEHYDRATED"...but Jesus said "I AM LIVING WATER."

I said, "I AM GOIN TO DIE"...but Jesus said "I WILL RAISE YOU UP."

I WILL NOT speak forth fear. **I will say and believe** *For God has not given ME a spirit of fear, but of power and of love and of a sound mind.* 2 Tim 1:7

I WILL NOT speak forth defeat. **I will say and believe** *"God always causes me to triumph in Christ Jesus."* 2 Cor 2:14

I WILL NOT speak forth "I can't". **I will say and believe** *"I can do all things through Christ who strengthens me".* Phil 4:13

I WILL NOT speak forth doubt. **I will say and believe** *"God has given to every man the measure of faith."* Rom 12:3

I WILL NOT speak forth lack. **I will say and believe** *"My God will supply all that I have need of according to His riches in glory by Christ Jesus."* Phil 4:1

I WILL NOT speak forth weakness. **I will say and believe** *"The Lord is the strength of my life."* Ps 27:1

I WILL NOT speak forth any supremacy of Satan over my life. **I will say and believe** *"Greater is Christ within me than Satan or unsaved man that is in the world."* 1 John 4:4

I WILL NOT speak forth sickness. **I will say and believe** *"With His stripes I am healed."* Isa 53:5

I WILL NOT speak forth bondage. **I will say and *believe*** *"Where the Spirit of the Lord is, there is freedom."* 2 Cor 3:17

I WILL NOT speak forth lack of wisdom. **I will say and believe** *"Christ Jesus is made unto me wisdom from God."* 1 Cor 1:30

I WILL NOT speak forth worries and frustrations. **I will say and believe** *"I Cast all my cares upon Hm who cares for me."* 1 Peter 5:7

I WILL NOT speak forth <u>condemnation</u>. **I will say and believe** *"There is no condemnation to any person in Christ Jesus."* Rom 8:1

I WILL NOT speak forth <u>a lie</u>. I will say and believe *"I have walked in Your truth."* Ps 26:3

I WILL NOT speak <u>loneliness</u>. I will say and believe *"I am with you always, even to the end of the age."* Matt 28:20; *"for You are with me"* Ps 23:4

I WILL NOT speak <u>oppression</u>. I will say and believe *"It was for freedom that Christ set us free; therefore keep standing firm and do not be subject again to a yoke of slavery."* Gal 5:1

I WIL NOT speak <u>pride.</u> I will say and believe *"Pride goes before destruction, And a haughty spirit before stumbling."* Prov 16:18

(All underlines are added by the author)

In Him

Acts 17:28 ... *for in Him we live and move and exist* (underlines by author)

John 15:5 *I am the vine, you are the branches; he who abides in Me and I in him, he bears much fruit...*

2 Cor 5:17-18 *Therefore if anyone is in Christ, he is a new creature; the old things passed away; behold, new things have come.*

1 Cor 1:30 *But by His doing you are in Christ Jesus, who became to us wisdom from God, and righteousness and sanctification, and redemption...*

Col 1:26-27...*the mystery which has been hidden from the past ages and generations, but has now been manifested to His saints, 27 ... which is Christ in you, the hope of glory.*

Gal 2:20 *I have been crucified with Christ; and it is no longer I who live, but Christ lives in me;*

Rom 8:1 *Therefore there is now no condemnation for those who are in Christ Jesus.*

Col 1:13-14 *13 For He rescued us from the domain of darkness and transferred us to the kingdom of His beloved Son, 14 in whom we have redemption, the forgiveness of sins.*

Eph 1:7 *In Him we have redemption through His blood, the forgiveness of our trespasses...*

Rom 8:2 *For the law of the Spirit of life in Christ Jesus has set you free from the law of sin and of death.*

HIDDEN IN CHRIST
Col 3:3 ...*your life is hidden with Christ in God.*

HIDDEN UNDER HIS WINGS
Ps 17:8 *Hide me in the shadow of Your wings*

Ps 57:1 *...in the shadow of Your wings I will take refuge*

Isa 49:2 *...In the shadow of His hand He has concealed Me; And He has also made Me a select arrow, He has hidden Me in His quiver.*

HID IN HIS PRESENCE (House)

Ps 27:5 *For in the day of trouble He will conceal me in His tabernacle; In the secret place of His tent He will hide me;*

Ps 91:1-2 *He who dwells in the shelter of the Most High Will abide in the shadow of the Almighty. 2 I will say to the Lord, "My refuge and my fortress..."*

EXPECT HIS PRESENCE IN YOUR LIFE

Ex 33:14-15 *My presence shall go with you, and I will give you rest.*

Ps 140:13 *The upright will dwell in Your presence.*

2 Chron 15:2 *...the Lord is with you when you are with Him. And if you seek Him, He will let you find Him.*

Deut 31:8 *It is the Lord Who goes before you; He will [march] with you; He will not fail you or let you go or forsake you;*

Matt 28:20 *I am with you always, even to the end of the age.*

John 15:5 *I am the vine, you are the branches; he who abides in Me and I in him...*

John 14:23-24 *If anyone loves Me, he will keep My word; and My Father will love him, and We will come to him and make Our abode with him.*

INTEGRITY

(Complete Truth, Reliability)

Ps 25:21 *Let integrity and uprightness preserve me…*

Ps 26:1 *Vindicate me, O Lord, for I have walked in my integrity, And I have trusted in the Lord without wavering.*

Ps 26:11 *But as for me, I shall walk in my integrity;*

Ps 41:12 *As for me, You uphold me in my integrity.*

Prov 11:3 *The integrity of the upright will guide them, But the crookedness of the treacherous will destroy them.*

1 Kings 9:4-5 *As for you, if you will walk before Me as your father David walked, in integrity of heart and uprightness, doing according to all that I have commanded you and will keep My statutes and My ordinances…*

Ps 101:2 *I will walk within my house with a perfect heart.* NKJV

Job 2:3 *…a blameless and upright man, one who fears God and shuns evil? And still he holds fast to his integrity, although you incited Me against him.* NKJV

Prov 20:7 *The righteous man walks in his integrity; His children are blessed after him.* NKJV

INTEREST (ON MONEY)

Ex 22:25 *If you lend money to any of My people who are poor among you, you shall not be like a moneylender to him; you shall not charge him interest.* NKJV (v. 26 says don't even take a garment as a pledge overnight.

Deut 23:19-20 *You shall not lend on interest to your brother — interest on money, on victuals, on anything that is lent for interest. 20 You may lend on interest to a foreigner, but to your brother you shall not lend on interest.* AMP (all right to charge interest to the stranger)

Ps 15:5 *[He who] does not put out his money for interest [to one of his own people]* AMP

Ezek 18:16 *...nor has taken anything in pledge.* AMP

Matt 25:27 *Then you should have invested my money with the bankers, and at my coming I would have received what was my own with interest.* AMP

Jer 15:10 *I have neither loaned, nor have men loaned to me...* AMP

Joy is a <u>choice</u> that you make. Grab hold and never lose your grip…you choose.

John 15:11 *I have told you these things, that My joy and delight may be in you, and that your joy and gladness may be of full measure and complete and overflowing.* AMP

Neh 8:10 *… the joy of the Lord is your strength. You must not be dejected and sad!* TLB

Phil 4:4 *Rejoice in the Lord always; again I will say, rejoice!*

THERE IS JOY IN SERVING GOD
Luke 10:17 *The seventy returned with joy,*

Luke 10:21 *At that very time He rejoiced greatly in the Holy Spirit,*

Luke 1:44-45 *For behold, when the sound of your greeting reached my ears, the baby leaped in my womb for joy.*

Ps 5:11 *But let all who take refuge in You be glad, Let them ever sing for joy;*

Ps 16:11 *You will make known to me the path of life; In Your presence is fullness of joy;*

Acts 16:34 *…and rejoiced greatly, having believed in God*

Ps 132:16-17 *…saints shall shout for joy.* TLB

Heb 1:9 *YOUR GOD, HAS ANOINTED YOU WITH THE OIL OF GLADNESS ABOVE YOUR COMPANIONS.*

Acts 2:46 *…they were taking their meals together with gladness and sincerity of heart,*

Gal 5:22-23 *But the fruit of the Spirit is love, joy, peace, patience, kindness, goodness, faithfulness, 23 gentleness, self-control...*

LACK OF JOY BRINGS MAJOR PROBLEMS

Deut 28:47-48 *Because you did not serve the Lord your God with joy and a glad heart, for the abundance of all things; 48 therefore you shall serve your enemies whom the Lord will send against you, in hunger, in thirst, in nakedness, and in the lack of all things; and He will put an iron yoke on your neck until He has destroyed you.*

Joel 1:12 *The vine dries up And the fig tree fails; The pomegranate, the palm also, and the apple tree, All the trees of the field dry up. Indeed, rejoicing dries up From the sons of men.*

THERE IS JOY IN THE MIDST OF TRIALS

Hab 3:17-18 *Though the fig tree does not blossom and there is no fruit on the vines, [though] the product of the olive fails and the fields yield no food, though the flock is cut off from the fold and there are no cattle in the stalls, 18 Yet I will rejoice in the Lord; I will exult in the [victorious] God of my salvation!* AMP

Rom 8:37-39 *Yet amid all these things we are more than conquerors and gain a surpassing victory through Him Who loved us. 38 For I am persuaded beyond doubt (am sure) that neither death nor life, nor angels nor principalities, nor things impending and threatening nor things to come, nor powers, 39 Nor height nor depth, nor anything else in all creation will be able to separate us from the love of God which is in Christ Jesus our Lord.* AMP

Ps 89:16 *In Your name they rejoice all the day...*

2 Cor 7:3-4 *Great is my confidence in you; great is my boasting on your behalf. I am filled with comfort; I am overflowing with joy in all our affliction.*

2 Cor 8:2 *For in the midst of an ordeal of severe tribulation, their abundance of joy and their depth of poverty [together] have overflowed in wealth of lavish generosity on their part.* AMP

Ps 30:5 *Weeping may endure for a night, but joy comes in the morning.* AMP

1 Thess 1:6 *And you [set yourselves to] become imitators of us and [through us] of the Lord Himself, for you welcomed our message in [spite of] much persecution, with joy [inspired] by the Holy Spirit;* AMP

1 Thess 5:18 *Thank [God] in everything [no matter what the circumstances may be, be thankful and give thanks], for this is the will of God for you [who are] in Christ Jesus [the Revealer and Mediator of that will].* AMP

James 1:2 *Consider it wholly joyful, my brethren, whenever you are enveloped in or encounter trials of any sort or fall into various temptations.* AMP

Luke 6:23 *Rejoice and be glad at such a time and exult and leap for joy...* AMP

Eph 5:20 *At all times and for everything giving thanks in the name of our Lord Jesus Christ to God the Father.* AMP

Ps 51:12 *Restore to me the joy of Your salvation.* AMP

JOY BRINGS DELIVERANCE
Prov 15:15 *...he who is of a merry heart has a continual feast.* NKJV

Prov 15:13 *A merry heart makes a cheerful countenance...* NKJV

Prov 17:22 *A merry heart does good, like medicine, But a broken spirit dries the bones.* NKJV

Neh 8:10 *Do not sorrow, for the joy of the Lord is your strength.* NKJV

Isa 12:3 *Therefore with joy you will draw water From the wells of salvation.* NKJV

Acts 16:25-26 *But at midnight Paul and Silas were praying and singing hymns to God, and the prisoners were listening to them...26 and immediately all the doors were opened and everyone's chains were loosed* (Paul and Silas rejoiced their way out of prison!) NKJV

JOY IS A COMMAND
Prov 5:18 *...rejoice with the wife of your youth.* NKJV

Eph 5:20 ...*giving thanks always for all things to God the Father in the name of our Lord Jesus Christ.* NKJV

1 Thess 5:18 ...*in everything give thanks; for this is the will of God in Christ Jesus for you.* NKJV

Prov 6:16-19 *These six things the Lord hates, Yes, seven are an abomination to Him: 17 A proud look, A lying tongue, Hands that shed innocent blood, 18 A heart that devises wicked plans, Feet that are swift in running to evil, 19 A false witness who speaks lies, And one who sows discord among brethren.* NKJV

Prov 12:22 *Lying lips are an abomination to the Lord, But those who deal truthfully are His delight.* NKJV

Ps 31:18 *Let the lying lips be put to silence...* NKJV

Ps 120:2 *Deliver my soul, O Lord, from lying lips And from a deceitful tongue.* NKJV

Prov 13:5 *A righteous man hates lying...* NKJV

Prov 15:4 *A wholesome tongue is a tree of life, But perverseness in it breaks the spirit.* NKJV

SOURCE OF LIES
John 8:44 *You are of your father the devil, and you want to do the desires of your father. He was a murderer from the beginning, and does not stand in the truth because there is no truth in him. Whenever he speaks a lie, he speaks from his own nature, for he is a liar and the father of lies.*

Gen 3:4 *The serpent said to the woman, "You surely will not die!"*

STAY AWAY FROM LIARS
1 Tim 6:5 *...useless wranglings of men of corrupt minds and destitute of the truth... From such withdraw yourself.* NKJV

PUT LYING AWAY
Col 3:8-9 *But now you also, put them all aside: anger, wrath, malice, slander, and abusive speech from your mouth. 9 Do not lie to one another, since you laid aside the old self with its evil practices.*

Eph 4:25 *Therefore, laying aside falsehood, SPEAK TRUTH EACH ONE of you WITH HIS NEIGHBOR...*

Eph 4:15 *...speaking the truth in love...*

RESULT OF LYING

Prov 19:9 *A false witness will not go unpunished, And he who tells lies will perish.*

Rev 21:8 *But for the cowardly and unbelieving and abominable and murderers and immoral persons and sorcerers and idolaters and all liars, their part will be in the lake that burns with fire and brimstone, which is the second death.*

SLANDER

Ps 101:5 *Whoever secretly slanders his neighbor, him I will destroy...*
(The Heb. word "lashan" means to use the tongue to defame, abuse, scandalize, or belittle the character of another.)

Rom 1:28-32 *...being filled with all unrighteousness...they are gossips, 30 slanderers,... untrustworthy,... 32 and although they know the ordinance of God, that those who practice such things are worthy of death.*

    3 causes of Slander:
        1. *Evil heart* (Lk6:45)
        2. *Hatred* (Ps 109:3)
        3. *Idleness* (1 Tim 5:13)
    6 results of Slander:
        1. *Friends separated* (Pro 16:28; 17:9)
        2. *Deadly wounds caused* (Pro 18:8; 26:22)
        3. *Strife* (Pro 26:20)
        4. *Discord among brethren* (Pro 6:19)
        5. *Anger (*Pro 25:23)
        6. *Murder* (Ps 31:13

LIVE

John 6:57 *Just as the living Father sent Me and I live by (through, because of) the Father...* AMP

Rom 1:17 *The man who through faith is just and upright shall live and shall live by faith.* AMP

Deut 30:19 *I call heaven and earth to witness this day against you that I have set before you life and death, the blessings and the curses; therefore choose life, that you and your descendants may live* AMP

LONELINESS

(The words loneliness and lonely, do not appear in the KJV).

John 14:16 *And I will ask the Father, and He will give you another Comforter (Counselor, Helper, Intercessor, Advocate, Strengthener, and Standby), that He may remain with you forever...* AMP

John 15:4 *Dwell in Me, and I will dwell in you. [Live in Me, and I will live in you.]* AMP

Heb 13:5 *Let your character or moral disposition be free from love of money [including greed, avarice, lust, and craving for earthly possessions] and be satisfied with your present [circumstances and with what you have]; for He [God] Himself has said, I will not in any way fail you nor give you up nor leave you without support. [I will] not, [I will] not, [I will] not in any degree leave you helpless nor forsake nor let [you] down (relax My hold on you)! [Assuredly not!].* AMP

Rom 8:38 *For I am persuaded beyond doubt (am sure)...nor anything...will be able to separate us from the love of God...* AMP

Ps 23:4 *...for You are with me...* AMP

John 8:29 *...My Father has not left Me alone...* AMP

John 16:32 *...I am not alone, because the Father is with Me.* AMP   skh

LONG LIFE

Ps 90:10 *The days of our years are threescore years and ten (seventy years)—or even, if by reason of strength, fourscore years (eighty years)...* AMP

Ps 91:16 *With long life will I satisfy him and show him My salvation.* AMP

Ps 92:14-15 *[Growing in grace] they shall still bring forth fruit in old age; they shall be full of sap [of spiritual vitality] and [rich in the] verdure [of trust, love, and contentment]. 15 [They are living memorials] to show that the Lord is upright and faithful to His promise.* AMP

Ps 118:17 *I shall not die but live, and shall declare the works and recount the illustrious acts of the Lord.* AMP

Ps 61:6 *You will prolong the king's life;*

Prov 3:2 *For length of days and years of life And peace they will add to you.*

Prov 3:16 *Length of days is in her right hand.* NKJV

Prov 9:11 *For by me your days will be multiplied, And years of life will be added to you.* NKJV

1 Kings 3:14 *So if you walk in My ways, to keep My statutes and My commandments, as your father David walked, then I will lengthen your days.* NKJV

Gen 25:8 *Then Abraham breathed his last and died in a good old age, an old man and full of years...* NKJV

> Five times a person is called "old man."
> 1. *Abraham* Gen 25:8
> 2. *Jacob* Gen 43:27
> 3. *An unnamed man of* Judg 19:16-22
> 4. *Eli* 1 Sam 4:18
> 5. *Zacharias* Luke 1:18

Gen 35:29 *So Isaac breathed his last and died, and was gathered to his people, being old and full of days.* NKJV

Isa 38:5 *"I have heard your prayer, I have seen your tears; surely I will add to your days* fifteen years..." NKJV

Isa 46:4 *Even to your old age...* NKJV

Job 42:17 *So Job died, old and full of days.* NKJV

Ps 21:4 *He asked life from You, and You gave it to him — Length of days forever and ever.* NKJV

LOVE

A STUDY

WHAT IS LOVE?

("Charity" in the KJV is the Gk "Agape" and refers to a God-type Love).

I Cor 13 *"Love endures long and is patient and kind; love never is envious nor boils over with jealousy; is not boastful or vainglorious, does not display itself haughtily. Love is not conceited--arrogant and inflated with pride; it is not rude and does not act unbecomingly. Love does not insist on its own rights or its own way, for it is not self-seeking; it is not touchy or fretful or resentful; it takes no account of the evil done to It, pays no attention to a suffered wrong. It does not rejoice at injustice and unrighteousness, but rejoices when right and truth prevail. Love bears up under anything and everything that comes, is ever ready to believe the best of every person, its hopes are fadeless under all circumstances and it endures everything. Love never fails."*

NINE INGREDIENTS OF LOVE:
1. *Patience*; no hurry, suffers long, believes, bears.
2. *Kindness*; love in action; never acts rashly, not inconsistent, puffed-up or proud.
3. *Generosity*; love in competition; not envious or jealous.
4. *Humility*; love in hiding; no parade, works then retires.
5. *Courtesy*; love in society; does not behave unseemly always polite, never rude or discourteous.
6. *Unselfishness*; love in essence; never selfish, sour or bitter. Does not retaliate or seek revenge.
7. *Good temper*; love in disposition; never irritated or resentful.
8. *Righteousness*; love in conduct; hates Sill, never glad when others go wrong. Always hopeful, glad.
9. *Sincerity*; love in profession; never boastful, not a hypocrite, always honest. Always just, and truthful. Knows how to be silent.

Luke 6:27-31 *"But I say to you who hear: Love your enemies, do good to those who hate you, 28 bless those who curse you, and pray for those who spitefully use you. 29 To him who strikes you on the one cheek, offer the other also. And from him who takes away your cloak, do not withhold your tunic either. 30 Give to* everyone who asks of you. And from him who takes away your goods do not ask them back. 31 And just as you want men to do to you, you also do to them likewise. NKJV

Jer 31:3 "Yes, I have loved you with an everlasting love; Therefore with lovingkindness I have drawn you." NKJV

1 John 4:16 *God is love, and he who abides in love abides in God, and God in him.* NKJV

1 John 4:12-13 *If we love one another, God abides in us, and His love has been perfected in us.* NKJV

Rom 8:39 *...height nor depth, nor any other created thing, shall be able to separate us from the love of God which is in Christ Jesus our Lord.* NKJV

John 15:10 *If you keep My commandments, you will abide in My love, just as I have kept My Father's commandments and abide in His love.* NKJV

Rom 5:5 *...the love of God has been poured out in our hearts by the Holy Spirit who was given to us.* NKJV

LOVE IS TO BE MANIFESTED IN GOD'S CHILDREN
Matt 5:44 *But I say to you, love your enemies, bless those who curse you, do good to those who hate you, and pray for those who spitefully use you and persecute you...* NKJV

Heb 10:24 *...let us consider how to stimulate one another to love and good deeds...*

1 Peter 1:22 *...fervently love one another from the heart...*

LOVE IS A COMMAND
John 15:12-13 *This is My commandment, that you love one another, just as I have loved you.*

John 13:34-35 *A new commandment I give to you, that you love one another, even as I have loved you, that you also love one another. 35 By this all men will know that you are My disciples, if you have love for one another.*

Matt 22:37-40 *And He said to him, "'YOU SHALL LOVE THE LORD YOUR GOD WITH ALL YOUR HEART, AND WITH ALL YOUR SOUL, AND WITH ALL YOUR MIND.' 38 This is the great and foremost commandment. 39 The second is like it, 'YOU SHALL LOVE YOUR NEIGHBOR AS YOURSELF.' 40 On these two commandments depend the whole Law and the Prophets."*

1 Cor 16:14 *Let all that you do be done in love.*

Col 3:14 *...above all these things put on love.*

LOVE FORGIVES
Ps 78:38 *But He, full of [merciful] compassion, forgave their iniquity and destroyed them not; yes, many a time He turned His anger away and did not stir up all His wrath and indignation.* AMP

LOVE RELEASES THE POWER OF GOD
1 John 2:10-11 *The one who loves his brother abides in Light and there is no cause for stumbling in him.*

Mark 1:41 *Moved with compassion, Jesus stretched out His hand and touched him, and said to him, "I am willing; be cleansed*

Matt 14:14 *When He went ashore, He saw a large crowd, and felt compassion for them and healed their sick.*

LOVE GIVES
John 12:25 *He who loves his life loses it, and he who hates his life in this world will keep it to life eternal.*

1 John 3:16 *We know love by this, that He laid down His life for us; and we ought to lay down our lives for the brethren.*

MEDITATION

A STUDY

MEDITATION ON GOD'S WORD IS A COMMAND

Ps 77:12 *I will meditate also upon all Your works and consider all Your [mighty] deeds.* AMP

Ps 119:78 *I will meditate on Your precepts.* AMP

1 Tim 4:15 *Meditate on these things; give yourself entirely to them...* NKJV

Ps 119:97 *Oh, how I love Your law! It is my meditation all the day.* NKJV

Josh 1:8 *This Book of the Law shall not depart from your mouth, but you shall meditate in it day and night, that you may observe to do according to all that is written in it.* NKJV

John 14:23 *Jesus answered and said to him, "If anyone loves Me, he will keep My word;*

2 Peter 3:1-3 *I now write to you this second epistle (in both of which I stir up your pure minds by way of reminder), 2 that you may be mindful of the words which were spoken before by the holy prophets, and of the commandment of us, the apostles of the Lord and Savior...* NKJV

MEDITATION ON GOD'S WORD BRINGS SUCCESS

Ps 1:2-3 *But his delight is in the law of the Lord, and on his law he meditates day and night. 3 He is like a tree planted by streams of water, which yields its fruit in season and whose leaf does not wither. Whatever he does prospers.* NIV

Prov 4:21-23 *Let them not depart from your sight; keep them in the center of your heart. 22 For they are life to those who find them, healing and health to all their flesh. 23 Keep and guard your heart with all vigilance and above all that you guard, for out of it flow the springs of life.* AMP

Ps 37:31 *The law of his God is in his heart; none of his steps shall slide.* AMP

2 Tim 2:7 *Think over these things I am saying [understand them and grasp their application], for the Lord will grant you full insight and understanding in everything.* AMP

Josh 1:8 *This Book of the Law shall not depart out of your mouth, but you shall meditate on it day and night, that you may observe and do according to all that is written in it. For then you shall make your way prosperous, and then you shall deal wisely and have good success.* AMP

MEDITATION ON PLEASANTRIES IS A COMMAND
Phil 4:8 *Finally, brethren, whatever is true, whatever is honorable, whatever is right, whatever is pure, whatever is lovely, whatever is of good repute, if there is any excellence and if anything worthy of praise, dwell on these things.*

Ps 145:5 *On the glorious splendor of Your majesty and on Your wondrous works I will meditate.* AMP

Ps 19:14 *Let the words of my mouth and the meditation of my heart Be acceptable in Your sight, O Lord, my rock and my Redeemer.*

Ps 49:3 *My mouth will speak wisdom, And the meditation of my heart will be understanding.*

MEDITATION IS A TIME OF QUIETNESS
Gen 24:63 *Isaac went out to meditate in the field toward evening.*

Acts 10:9 *On the next day, as they were on their way and approaching the city, Peter went up on the housetop about the sixth hour to pray.*

Ps 77:6 *I will remember my song in the night; I will meditate with my heart, And my spirit ponders.*

Num 9:8 *Stand still, and I will hear what the Lord will command concerning you.* KJV

Ps 46:10 *Be still, and know that I am God...* KJV

Ps 63:6 *When I remember You upon my bed and meditate on You in the night watches.* AMP

Meekess and Humility

Ps 147:6 *The Lord lifts up the humble and downtrodden;* AMP

Isa 29:19 *The meek also shall increase their joy in the Lord...* AMP

Matt 5:5 *"Blessed are the gentle, for they shall inherit the earth."*

Matt 11:29 *Take My yoke upon you and learn from Me, for I am gentle and humble in heart, and YOU WILL FIND REST FOR YOUR SOULS.*

Gal 5:22-23 *But the fruit of the Spirit is love, joy, peace, patience, kindness, goodness, faithfulness, 23 gentleness, self-control; against such things there is no law.*

Gal 6:1 *Brethren, even if anyone is caught in any trespass, you who are spiritual, restore such a one in a spirit of gentleness;*

2 Tim 2:24-25 *And a servant of the Lord must not quarrel but be gentle to all, able to teach, patient, 25 in humility correcting those who are in opposition...* NKJV

Eph 4:1-2 T*herefore I, the prisoner of the Lord, implore you to walk in a manner worthy of the calling with which you have been called, 2 with all humility and gentleness, with patience, showing tolerance for one another in love.*

Num 12:3-4 *(Now the man Moses was very humble, more than any man who was on the face of the earth.)*

Ps 149:4 *For the Lord takes pleasure in His people; He will beautify the humble with salvation.* NKJV

Ps 25:9 *He leads the humble in what is right, and the humble He teaches His way.* AMP

MIND, Renewal of the
A STUDY

Rom 12:2 *And do not be conformed to this world, but be transformed by the renewing of your mind...*

YOUR MIND HAS BEEN PERVERTED FROM YOUTH

Gen 6:5 *Then the Lord saw that the wickedness of man was great on the earth, and that every intent of the thoughts of his heart was only evil continually.*

Gen 8:21 *I will never again curse the ground on account of man, for the intent of man's heart is evil from his youth;*

Eph 2:2-3...*you formerly walked according to the course of this world, according to the prince of the power of the air, of the spirit that is now working in the sons of disobedience. 3 Among them we too all formerly lived in the lusts of our flesh, indulging the desires of the flesh and of the mind.*

Ps 10:4 *The wicked in his proud countenance does not seek God;* God is in none of his thoughts. NKJV

Ps 94:11 *The Lord knows the thoughts of man, That they are futile.* NKJV

Prov 15:26 *The thoughts of the wicked are an abomination to the Lord.* NKJV

Isa 55:6-7 *Seek the Lord while He may be found, Call upon Him while He is near. 7 Let the wicked forsake his way, And the unrighteous man his thoughts;* NKJV

THE MIND OF CHRIST IS RECEIVED WHEN YOU ARE BORN-AGAIN

1 Cor 2:16 *But we have the mind of Christ.* NKJV

THIS MIND MUST BE ACTIVATED BY YOU

Phil 2:5 *Let this mind be in you which was also in Christ Jesus...* NKJV

Eph 4:23-24 ...*be renewed in the spirit of your mind, 24 and that you put on the new man which was created according to God, in true righteousness and holiness.* NKJV

Col 3:9-11 *Do not lie to one another, since you have put off the old man with his deeds, 10 and have put on the new man who is renewed in knowledge according to the image of Him who created him...* NKJV

Heb 6:10-11 *For God is not unjust so as to forget your work and the love which you have shown toward His name, in having ministered and in still ministering to the saints.*

Heb 13:15 *...give thanks to His name.*

James 5:14 *...anointing him with oil in the name of the Lord;*

1 Peter 4:14 *If you are insulted because of the name of Christ, you are blessed, for the Spirit of glory and of God rests on you.* NIV

1 John 2:12 *I am writing to you, little children, because your sins have been forgiven you for His name's sake.*

1 John 3:23 *This is His commandment, that we believe in the name of His Son Jesus Christ,*

1 John 5:13 *These things I have written to you who believe in the name of the Son of God, so that you may know that you have eternal life.*

Ps 44:5 *...through Your name shall we tread them under who rise up against us.* AMP

Isa 12:4 *And in that day you will say, Give thanks to the Lord, call upon His name and by means of His name [in solemn entreaty]; declare and make known His deeds among the peoples of the earth, proclaim that His name is exalted!* AMP

Rev 19:12-14 *His eyes were like a flame of fire, and on His head were many crowns. He had a name written that no one knew except Himself. 13 He was clothed with a robe dipped in blood, and His name is called The Word of God.* NKJV

Rev 19:16 *And He has on His robe and on His thigh a name written: KING OF KINGS AND LORD OF LORDS.* NKJV

THE OLD TESTAMENT THREAD of Jesus

In Genesis, He is *the Seed*

In Exodus, *The Passover Lamb*

In Leviticus, *the High Priest*

In Numbers, *A Pillar of fire by night, A Pillar of Cloud by Day*

In Deuteronomy, *He's the Prophet*

In Joshua, the *Captain of our Salvation*

In Judges, the *Judge and Lawgiver*

He's our *Redeemer* in Ruth

Our *Trusted Prophet* in Samuel

And in Kings & Chronicles, *He's our Reigning King!*

In Ezra, He's revealed as a *rebuilder of the broken-down walls of human life*

In Job, He's our *Everlasting Redeemer*

In Psalms, our *Shepherd*

In Proverbs and Ecclesiastes, our *Wisdom*

In Song of Solomon, He's our *Lover and Bridegroom*

Our *Prince of Peace* in Isaiah

And *Righteous Branch* in Jeremiah

In Lamentations our *unfailing compassion*

In Ezekiel the *eternal Messiah who reigns*

In Daniel, He's the *4th man in a fiery furnace* In Hosea the *Redeemer*

In Joel, *He's the Baptism with the Holy Ghost and Fire!*

He's the *Burden Barer* of Amos

The *Mighty One* of Obadiah

In Jonah the *deliverer*

And in Micah, the *Majesty and Glory of God!*

In Nahum, *He's the All Powerful One*

In Habakkuk the *God of Glory and Greatness*

In Zephaniah, *He's Savior*

In Haggai, the *Restorer*

In Zechariah the *reigning King*

And in Malachi, *the Son of Righteousness with healing in His Wings!*

BECAUSE OF THE NAME OF JESUS

1. Because *"God hath highly exalted him, and given him the name which is above every name"* in heaven, earth, and hell (Philippians 2:9-11), I boldly speak His name in subduing all other names.

2. Because *"whatever you ask in My name, that I will do, that the Father may be glorified in the Son. If you ask anything in My name, I will do it"* NKJV (John 14:13-14), I confidently speak in His name, that the Father might be glorified.

3. Because *"If I ask any thing in His name, He will do it"* (John 14: 14), I know that anything includes salvation; healing, supply of needs, and liberation.

4. Because *"Whatsoever I ask the Father in Jesus' name, He will give it to me"* (John 16:23), I pray always to my Father in the name of His beloved Son.

5. Because He said, *"Until now you have asked nothing in My name. Ask, and you will receive, that your joy may be full"* NKJV (John 16:24), my joy is overflowing because of great and mighty answers.

6. With Peter, I fearlessly declare, *"In the name of Jesus Christ of Nazareth, rise up and walk"* NKJV (Acts 3:6)

7. Because *"on the basis of faith in His name, it is the name of Jesus...has given him this perfect health in the presence of you all"* (Acts 3:16), I confess childlike faith in Jesus' name.

8. *"Whatever you do [no matter what it is] in word or deed, do everything in the name of the Lord Jesus and in [dependence upon] His Person, giving praise to God the Father through Him"* AMP (Colossians 3: 17).

9. Because *"In the name of Jesus I cast out demons"* (Mark 16: 17) therefore I possess total authority over the works of Satan.

10. *"I give thanks always for all things unto God in the name of the Lord Jesus Christ"* (Ephesians 5:20).

11. I do not use the name of Jesus as a fetish or charm; I' know His name represents *"all 'power in heaven and in earth"* (Matthew 28: 18).

12. All hail the power of Jesus' name" is more than "an anthem; I hail the power of His saving, healing, delivering name...the matchless name of Jesus.

Gal 5:1-2 *Stand fast therefore in the liberty by which Christ has made us free, and do not be entangled again with a yoke of bondage.* NKJV

John 8:36 *Therefore if the Son makes you free, you shall be free indeed.* NKJV

TAKE YOUR FREEDOM FROM OPPRESSION
Eph 6:10 *...be strong in the Lord...* NKJV

Eph 4:27 *...and do not give the devil an opportunity.*

Col 1:13 *For He rescued us from the domain of darkness.*

Luke 10:19-20 *Behold, I have given you authority to tread on serpents and scorpions, and over all the power of the enemy, and nothing will injure you.*

RESIST THE DEVIL
1 Peter 5:8-9 *Be of sober spirit, be on the alert. Your adversary, the devil, prowls around like a roaring lion, seeking someone to devour. 9 But resist him, firm in your faith...*

James 4:7 *Submit therefore to God. Resist the devil and he will flee from you.*

HAVE A LOVING SPIRIT
Matt 5:44 *But I say to you, love your enemies and pray for those who persecute you...*

Col 3:14 *Beyond all these things put on love, which is the perfect bond of unity.*

Prov 10:12 *Hatred stirs up strife, But love covers all transgressions.*

HAVE A FORGIVING SPIRIT
Mark 11:25 *Whenever you stand praying, forgive, if you have anything against anyone, so that your Father who is in heaven will also forgive you your transgressions.*

Ps 5:11 *...let those also who love Your name be joyful in You and be in high spirits.* AMP

Ps 9:2 *I will rejoice in You and be in high spirits.* AMP

HAVE A TENDER SPIRIT
Isa 53:2 *For He grew up before Him like a tender shoot...*

AVAIL YOURSELF OF THE BLOOD OF JESUS
Rev 12:11 *And they overcame him because of the blood of the Lamb and because of the word of their testimony,* (by the Word of God which is in your testimony!)

FORSAKE ALL SIN
John 8:11 *From now on sin no more.*

John 5:14 *...do not sin anymore, so that nothing worse happens to you.*

1 John 4:4 *Little children, you are of God [you belong to Him] and have [already] defeated and overcome them [the agents of the antichrist], because He Who lives in you is greater (mightier) than he who is in the world.* AMP

1 John 5:4 *For whatever is born of God is victorious over the world; and this is the victory that conquers the world, even our faith.* AMP

Rom 8:37 *Yet amid all these things we are more than conquerors and gain a surpassing victory through Him Who loved us.* AMP

Rev 12:11 *And they have overcome (conquered) him by means of the blood of the Lamb and by the utterance of their testimony...* AMP

Ps 118:6 *The Lord is on my side; I will not fear. What can man do to me? [Heb 13:6.]* AMP

Ps 27:1 *THE LORD is my Light and my Salvation — whom shall I fear or dread? The Lord is the Refuge and Stronghold of my life — of whom shall I be afraid?* AMP skh

Peace

A STUDY

Eph 6:14 *...you will need the strong belt of truth...* TLB

Rom 5:1 *Therefore, having been justified by faith, we have peace with God through our Lord Jesus Christ.*

John 16:33 *These things I have spoken to you, so that in Me you may have peace.*

Ps 37:11 *But the meek shall inherit the earth, And shall delight themselves in the abundance of peace.*
NKJV

Ps 29:11 *The Lord will bless His people with peace.* NKJV

John 14:27 *Peace I leave with you, My peace I give to you...*NKJV

BE LED BY PEACE
Rom 14:19 *...let us pursue the things which make for peace and the things by which one may edify another.* NKJV

Col 3:15 *And let the peace of God rule in your hearts...* NKJV

Phil 4:7 *...and the peace of God, which surpasses all understanding, will guard your hearts and minds through Christ Jesus.* NKJV

Isa 55:12 *For you shall go out [from the spiritual exile caused by sin and evil into the homeland] with joy and be led forth [by your Leader, the Lord Himself, and His word] with peace;* AMP

GOD IS THE SOURCE OF PEACE
Rom 15:13 *May the God of your hope so fill you with all joy and peace in believing [through the experience of your faith] that by the power of the Holy Spirit you may abound and be overflowing (bubbling over) with hope.* AMP

2 Thess 3:16 *Now may the Lord of peace Himself grant you His peace (the peace of His kingdom) at all times and in all ways [under all circumstances and conditions, whatever comes]...* AMP

Eph 2:14 *For He Himself is our peace...*

1 Kings 2:33-34 *...to David and his descendants and his house and his throne, may there be peace from the Lord forever.*

Isa 26:3 *The steadfast of mind You will keep in perfect peace...*

THE WORD PRODUCES PEACE
Ps 119:165 *Those who love Your law have great peace...*

Mark 4:39 *And He got up and rebuked the wind and said to the sea, "Hush, be still." And the wind died down and it became perfectly calm.*

Prov 3:1-2 *...keep my commandments; 2 For length of days and years of life And peace they will add to you.*

PEACE DRIVES OUT FEAR
Gen 43:23 *"Peace be with you, do not be afraid..."* NKJV

Mal 2:5 *"My covenant was with him, one of life and peace..."* NKJV

Prov 14:31 *A calm and undisturbed mind and heart are the life and health of the body, but envy, jealousy, and wrath are like rottenness of the bones.* AMP

Isa 54:10 *For though the mountains should depart and the hills be shaken or removed, yet My love and kindness shall not depart from you, nor shall My covenant of peace and completeness be removed, says the Lord, Who has compassion on you.* AMP

Jer 33:6 *Behold, [in the future restored Jerusalem] I will lay upon it health and healing, and I will cure them and will reveal to them the abundance of peace (prosperity, security, stability) and truth.* AMP

2 Thess 3:16 *Now may the Lord of peace Himself grant you His peace (the peace of*

His kingdom) at all times and in all ways [under all circumstances and conditions, whatever comes]. AMP

Phil 4:11 *...for I have learned how to be content (satisfied to the point where I am not disturbed or disquieted) in whatever state I am.* AMP

Prov 3:7-8 *Be not wise in your own eyes; reverently fear and worship the Lord and turn [entirely] away from evil.] 8 It shall be health to your nerves and sinews, and marrow and moistening to your bones.* AMP

Gal 5:22 *But the fruit of the Spirit is love, joy, peace...* NKJV

Prov 15:15 *But he who is of a merry heart has a continual feast...* NKJV

Heb 12:14 *Pursue peace with all people...* NKJV

Matt 5:9 *Blessed are the peacemakers, For they shall be called sons of God.* NKJV

Rom 12:18 *If it is possible, as much as depends on you, live peaceably with all men.* NKJV

PEACE OF MIND skh
Rom 12:2 *And do not be conformed to this world, but be transformed by the renewing of your mind, so that you may prove what the will of God is, that which is good and acceptable and perfect.*

1 Cor 1:30 Christ Jesus, who became to us wisdom from God, and righteousness and sanctification, and redemption

2 Cor 10:5 *Inasmuch as we] refute arguments and theories and reasonings and every proud and lofty thing that sets itself up against the [true] knowledge of God; and we lead every thought and purpose away captive into the obedience of Christ (the Messiah, the Anointed One)...* AMP

2 Tim 1:7 *For God did not give us a spirit of timidity (of cowardice, of craven and cringing and fawning fear), but [He has given us a spirit] of power and of love and of calm and well-balanced mind and discipline and self-control.* AMP

Isa 26:3 *You will guard him and keep him in perfect and constant peace whose mind [both its inclination and its character] is stayed on You, because he commits himself to You, leans on You, and hopes confidently in You.* AMP

Ps 119:99 *I have better understanding and deeper insight than all my teachers, because Your testimonies are my meditation.* AMP

2 Tim 2:7 *Think over these things I am saying [understand them and grasp their application], for the Lord will grant you full insight and understanding in everything.* AMP

1 Peter 5:7 *Casting the whole of your care [all your anxieties, all your worries, all your concerns, once and for all] on Him, for He cares for you affectionately and cares about you watchfully.* AMP

Ps 55:22 *Cast your burden on the Lord [releasing the weight of it] and He will sustain you; He will never allow the [consistently] righteous to be moved (made to slip, fall, or fail).* AMP

Prov 16:3 *Roll your works upon the Lord [commit and trust them wholly to Him; He will cause your thoughts to become agreeable to His will, and] so shall your plans be established and succeed.* AMP

Prov 6:20-22 *My son, keep your father's [God-given] commandment and forsake not the law of [God] your mother [taught you]. [Eph 6:1-3.] 21 Bind them continually upon your heart and tie them about your neck. [Prov 3:3; 7:3.] 22 When you go, they [the words of your parents' God] shall lead you; when you sleep, they shall keep you; and when you waken, they shall talk with you.* AMP

Phil 4:8 *...whatever is true, whatever is worthy of reverence and is honorable and seemly, whatever is just, whatever is pure, whatever is lovely and lovable, whatever is kind and winsome and gracious, if there is any virtue and excellence, if there is anything worthy of praise, think on and weigh and take account of these things [fix your minds on them].* AMP

Isa 54:13 *...great shall be the peace and undisturbed composure of your children* AMP

Isa 55:12 *For you shall go out [from the spiritual exile caused by sin and evil into* the homeland] with joy and be led forth [by your Leader, the Lord Himself, and His word] with peace; AMP

Phil 4:6-7 *Do not fret or have any anxiety about anything, but in every circumstance and in everything, by prayer and petition (definite requests), with thanksgiving, continue to make your wants known to God. 7 And God's peace [shall be yours, that tranquil state of a soul assured of its salvation through Christ, and so fearing nothing from God and being content with its earthly lot of whatever sort that is, that peace] which transcends all understanding shall garrison and mount guard over your hearts and minds in Christ Jesus.* AMP

Col 3:15 *And let the peace (soul harmony which comes) from Christ rule (act as umpire continually) in your hearts [deciding and settling with finality all questions that arise in your minds, in that peaceful state].* AMP

Eph 4:23 *And be constantly renewed in the spirit of your mind [having a fresh mental and spiritual attitude]...* AMP

Prov 15:15 *All the days of the desponding and afflicted are made evil [by anxious thoughts and forebodings], but he who has a glad heart has a continual feast [regardless of circumstances].* AMP

Phil 4:11 *I have learned how to be content (satisfied to the point where I am not disturbed or disquieted) in whatever state I am.* AMP

Eph 2:14 *For He is [Himself] our peace.* AMP

Prov 14:30 *A calm and undisturbed mind and heart are the life and health of the body, but envy, jealousy, and wrath are like rottenness of the bones.* AMP

Ps 29:11 *...the Lord will bless His people with peace.* AMP

John 14:27 *Peace I leave with you; My [own] peace I now give and bequeath to you.* AMP

POVERTY

A STUDY

POVERTY COMES TO THOSE WHO ARE LAZY

Prov 20:13 *Do not love sleep, lest you come to poverty;* NKJV

Prov 20:4 *The lazy man will not plow because of winter; He will beg during harvest and have nothing.* NKJV

POVERTY COMES TO THOSE WHO IGNORE INSTRUCTION

Prov 13:18 *Poverty and shame will come to him who neglects discipline.*

Matt 6:33 *But seek first His kingdom and His righteousness, and all these things will be added to you.*

POVERTY COMES TO THE SELFISH

Prov 12:9 *Better is the one who is slighted but has a servant, Than he who honors himself but lacks bread.* NKJV

Prov 11:24 *There is one who scatters, yet increases more; And there is one who withholds more than is right, But it leads to poverty.* NKJV

Prov 10:4 *He who has a slack hand becomes poor, But the hand of the diligent makes rich.* NKJV

POVERTY IS NOT FOR GOD'S CHILDREN

Ps 37:25 *I have been young and now I am old, Yet I have not seen the righteous forsaken Or his descendants begging bread.*

Ps 34:10 *...they who seek the Lord shall not be in want of any good thing.*

Ps 23:1 *The Lord is my shepherd, I shall not want.*

1 Sam 2:8 *He raises the poor from the dust, He lifts the needy from the ash heap To make them sit with nobles, And inherit a seat of honor; For the pillars of the earth are the Lord's, And He set the world on them.*

Luke 4:18 *"THE SPIRIT OF THE LORD IS UPON ME, BECAUSE HE ANOINTED ME TO PREACH THE GOSPEL TO THE POOR.* (and good news to the poor is not 'I want you to stay poor') ... *to preach deliverance to the captives .... to set at liberty them that are bruised."*

GOD'S WAY WOULD BE TO ELIMINATE POVERTY

Phil 4:19-20 *And my God will supply all your needs according to His riches in glory in Christ Jesus.*

Ps 37:4 *Delight yourself in the Lord; And He will give you the desires of your heart.*

Judg 18:10 *"When you enter, you will come to a secure people with a spacious land; for God has given it into your hand, a place where there is no lack of anything that is on the earth."*

PRAISE

A STUDY

Ps 57:7-9 My heart is steadfast, O God, my heart is steadfast; I will sing, yes, I will sing praises! 8 Awake, my glory! Awake, harp and lyre! I will awaken the dawn. 9 I will give thanks to You, O Lord, among the peoples; I will sing praises to You among the nations.

Ps 33:1-3 Sing for joy in the Lord, O you righteous ones; Praise is becoming to the upright. 2 Give thanks to the Lord with the lyre; Sing praises to Him with a harp of ten strings. 3 Sing to Him a new song;

Ps 147:1 Praise the Lord! For it is good to sing praises to our God; For it is pleasant and praise is becoming.

PRAISE GOD CONTINUALLY

Ps 34:1-2 I will bless the Lord at all times; His praise shall continually be in my mouth. 2 My soul will make its boast in the Lord;

Ps 71:6 My praise is continually of You.

Ps 71:8 My mouth is filled with Your praise And with Your glory all day long.

Ps 113:3 From the rising of the sun to its setting The name of the Lord is to be praised.

Ps 119:164 Seven times a day I praise You, Because of Your righteous ordinances.

THE NEW TESTAMENT CHURCH PRACTICED PRAISE

Acts 2:47 *... praising God and having favor with all the people.*

Luke 24:53 *...and were continually in the temple praising God.*

Heb 13:15-16 *...let us continually offer up a sacrifice of praise to God, that is, the fruit of lips that give thanks to His name.*

Acts 3:8 *...he entered the temple with them, walking and leaping and praising God.*

PRAISE GLORIFIES THE LORD
Ps 50:23 *He who offers a sacrifice of thanksgiving honors Me;*

PRAISE HIM REGARDLESS OF FEELING
Hab 3:17-18 *Though...there be no fruit on the vines...And the fields produce no food, And there be no cattle in the stalls... 18 ...I will rejoice in the God of my salvation.*

1 Thess 5:16-17 *Rejoice always; 17 pray without ceasing...*

PRAISE BRINGS GOD TO YOU
Ps 65:1 *Praise waiteth for thee, O God...* KJV

Ps 22:3 *You are holy, O You who are enthroned upon the praises of Israel.*

PRAISE BRINGS VICTORY
Ps 106:47 *Save us, O Lord our God, and gather us from among the heathen, to give thanks unto thy holy name, and to triumph in thy praise.* KJV

2 Chron 20:22 *And when they began to sing and to praise, the Lord set ambushments against the children of Ammon... and they were smitten.* KJV

Josh 6:20 *So the people shouted when the priests blew with the trumpets: and it came to pass, when the people heard the sound of the trumpet, and the people shouted with a great shout, that the wall fell down flat...* KJV

Acts 16:25-26 *And at midnight Paul and Silas prayed, and sang praises unto God...and immediately all the doors were opened, and every one's bands were loosed.* KJV

Luke 17:15, 19 *And one of them, when he saw that he was healed, turned back, and with a loud voice glorified God...19 thy faith hath made thee whole.* KJV

ABSENCE OF PRAISE IS A SIGN OF DEATH!
Ps 150:6 *Let every thing that hath breath praise the Lord. Praise ye the Lord.* KJV

Ps 115:17-18 *The dead praise not the Lord, neither any that go down into silence. 18 But we will bless the Lord from this time forth and for evermore. Praise the Lord.* KJV

Isa 38:18-19 *For the grave cannot praise thee, death can not celebrate thee: they that go down into the pit cannot hope for thy truth.19 The living, the living, he shall praise thee, as I do this day...* KJV

SEVEN HEBREW WORDS FOR PRAISE
1. 2 Chron 20:19 *The Levites...stood up to praise (HALAL) the Lord God of Israel, with a very loud voice.*
> **HALAL:** To celebrate, to boast, to rave, to be clamorously foolish.

2. Ps 50:23 *Whoso offereth praise (TOWDAH) glorifieth me...* KJV
> **TOWDAH:** To extend the hand in thanksgiving.

3. Ps 63:3 *Because thy lovingkindness is better than life, my lips shall praise (SHABACH) thee.* KJV
> **SHABACH:** To address in a loud tone, to shout.

4. Ps 72:15 *...and daily shall he be praised (BARAK).* KJV
> **BARAK:** To bless, to bow down in worship, expecting to receive something from Him.

5. Ps 57:7 *My heart is fixed, O God, my heart is fixed: I will sing and give praise (ZAMAR).* KJV
> **ZAMAR:** To rejoice in music before the Lord.

6. Ps 22:3 *But thou art holy, O thou that inhabitest the praises (TEHILLAH) of Israel.*
KJV
> **TEHILLAH:** To sing your HALAL; a song from your spirit.

7. Ps 134:2 *Lift up your hands in the sanctuary, and bless (YADAH) the Lord.*
KJV
> **YADAH:** To worship with extended hands. Similar to #2.

Praise is both personal and corporate. Your personality greatly influences your praise and worship. It is important for you to be comfortable. Be open to God as you grow in your praise of Him. The Bible has many illustrations in types of praise. Whatever you do, enjoy your praise of our Father!

SINGING

Ps 47:6-8 *Sing praises to God, sing praises; Sing praises to our King, sing praises. 7 For God is the King of all the earth; Sing praises with a skillful psalm. 8 God reigns over the nations...*

Ps 105:2 *Sing to Him, sing praises to Him;*

Ps 105:43 *And he brought forth his people with joy, and his chosen with gladness* (Heb for singing). KJV

Ps 146:2 *While I live will I praise the Lord: I will sing praises unto my God while I have any being.* KJV

Ps 104:3 *I will sing unto the Lord as long as I live: I will sing praise to my God while I have my being.* KJV

Ps 147:1 *Praise the Lord! For it is good to sing praises to our God; For it is pleasant and praise is becoming.*

- 2 Chron 29:27-28 *When the burnt offering began, the song to the Lord also began with the trumpets, accompanied by the instruments of David, king of Israel.*

- Ps 33:3 *Sing to Him a new song; Play skillfully with a shout of joy.*

- Ps 96:1-2 *Sing to the Lord a new song; Sing to the Lord, all the earth. 2 Sing to the Lord, bless His name; Proclaim good tidings of His salvation from day to day.*

- There were 7 new song in the Old Testament. The New Testament records 2. (Rev 5:9; 19:3)

CLAP YOUR HANDS

2 Kings 11:12 *...they clapped their hands...*

Ps 47:1 *O clap your hands, all peoples...*

SHOUT UNTO THE LORD
Ps 47:1 *O clap your hands, all peoples; Shout to God with the voice of joy.*
Ps 132:9 *And let Your godly ones sing for joy.*

Josh 6:5 *...when you hear the sound of the trumpet, all the people shall shout with a great shout; and the wall of the city will fall down flat.*

Zech 4:7 *'What are you, O great mountain? Before Zerubbabel you will become a plain; and he will bring forth the top stone with shouts of "Grace, grace to it!"'*

Isa 12:6 *...shout for joy, O inhabitant of Zion, For great in your midst is the Holy One of Israel.*

1 Thess 4:16 *For the Lord Himself will descend from heaven with a shout...*

DANCING
Ps 149:3 *Let them praise His name with dancing;*

Ps 150:4 *Praise Him with timbrel and dancing;*

Ps 30:11 *You have turned for me my mourning into dancing;*

Jer 31:13 *At that time young women will dance and be glad. The* NET Bible

2 Sam 6:14 *...and David was dancing before the Lord with all his might.*

- Heb 1:9 *"THEREFORE GOD, YOUR GOD, HAS ANOINTED YOU WITH THE OIL OF GLADNESS* (Gk.: leaping joy) *ABOVE YOUR COMPANIONS."*

- Acts 16:34 ... *and he leaped much for joy...* AMP

- Luke 6:23 *Rejoice and be glad at such a time and exult and leap for joy.* AMP

1 Sam 18:6 *...the women came out of all the Israelite towns, singing and dancing...*

AMP

Jer 31:4 *Again you will take up your tambourines, And go forth to the dances of the merrymakers.*
1 Sam 21:11 *Did they not sing of this one as they danced?*
Luke 10:21 *Jesus rejoiced in spirit* (To leap for joy). KJV

INSTRUMENTS
2 Chron 29:28 *And all the congregation worshiped, the singers sang, and the trumpeters sounded;* AMP

Ps 98:6 *With trumpets and the sound of the horn make a joyful noise before the King, the Lord!* AMP

1 Chron 15:28 *Thus all Israel brought up the ark of the covenant of the Lord with shouting, sound of the cornet, trumpets, and cymbals, sounding aloud with harps and lyres.* AMP

Ps 150:3-5 *Praise Him with trumpet sound; praise Him with lute and harp! 4 Praise Him with tambourine and [single or group] dance; praise Him with stringed and wind instruments or flutes! 5 Praise Him with resounding cymbals; praise Him with loud clashing cymbals!* AMP

Ps 81:2-3 *Raise a song, sound the timbrel, the sweet lyre with the harp. 3 Blow the trumpet at the New Moon, at the full moon, on our feast day.* AMP

1 Sam 18:6 *As they were coming home, when David returned from killing the Philistine, the women came out of all the Israelite towns, singing and dancing, to meet King Saul with timbrels, songs of joy, and instruments of music.* AMP

Ps 150:4-5 *Praise Him with tambourine and [single or group] dance; praise Him with stringed and wind instruments or flutes! 5 Praise Him with resounding cymbals; praise Him with loud clashing cymbals!* AMP

Additional use of musical instruments in the Bible:
1. Used by the prophets when prophesying (1 Sam 10:5)
2. David used them to remove a demon (1 Sam 16:16-23)
3. The righteous are commanded to use them in worship (Ps 33:1-5; 149:1-4; 150:1-6)

4.   It was a law of God (Ps 1:1-4; 2 Chr 29:25)
5.   It was a good thing (Ps 92:1-5)
6.   Called holy when dedicated to God (Num 31:6)
7.   Called instruments of God (1 Chr 16:42)
8.   God's glory came down when used (2 Chr 5:11-14)
9.   Elders and angels play them in heaven (Rev 5:8)
10.   Jews will play harps in heaven (Rev 14:1-5)
11.   Tribulation saints will play harps in heaven (Rev 15:2)
12.   The N.T. commands their use in the church (Eph 5:19; Col 3:16; Jas 5:13)

LIFT UP HANDS

Ps 63:4 *So will I bless You while I live; I will lift up my hands in Your name.* AMP

Ps 119:48 *My hands also will I lift up [in fervent supplication] to Your commandments, which I love, and I will meditate on Your statutes.* AMP

1 Tim 2:8 *Therefore I want the men in every place to pray, lifting up holy hands, without wrath and dissension.*

Deut 32:40 *Indeed, I lift up My hand to heaven,*

Lam 2:19 *Lift up your hands to Him...*

PRAYER

A STUDY

Ps 109:4 ...*but I give myself unto prayer.* KJV

HE HEARS MY PRAYER
Ps 4:3 ...*the Lord will hear when I call unto him.* KJV

Ps 55:17 *Evening, and morning, and at noon, will I pray, and cry aloud: and he shall hear my voice.* KJV

Ps 5:1-3 *O Lord, consider my meditation.2 Hearken unto the voice of my cry, my King, and my God: for unto thee will I pray.3 My voice shalt thou hear in the morning, O Lord; in the morning will I direct my prayer unto thee, and will look up.* KJV

2 Chron 7:14 *If my people, which are called by my name, shall humble themselves, and pray, and seek my face, and turn from their wicked ways; then will I hear from heaven, and will forgive their sin, and will heal their land.* KJV

Prov 15:29 *The Lord is far from the wicked: but he heareth the prayer of the righteous.* KJV

Isa 65:24 *And it shall come to pass, that before they call, I will answer; and while they are yet speaking, I will hear.* KJV

Rev 5:8 ...*which are the prayers of God's people (the saints).* AMP

I BEGIN EACH DAY WITH MY FATHER
Isa 26:9 ...*by my spirit within me I will seek You early;* NKJV

Ps 5:3 *My voice You shall hear in the morning, O Lord; In the morning I will direct it to You, And I will look up.* NKJV

There are 221 prayers recorded in the Bible! Not references TO prayer, rather 221 actual prayers (176 in the O.T. and 45 in the N.T.). The first one was Abraham recorded in Genesis 15:2-3 and the last one in Revelation 22:20. 36 of the 66 books in the Bible do not have a prayer recorded (including Proverbs, Ephesians, James, Hebrews and both books of Thessalonians and both of Timothy. The most prayers of any book are found in Psalms (72).

Ephesians chapter 3 pattern for prayer:
Pray for: 1. Spiritual power in the inner man, v16
2. Indwelling of Christ, v17
3. To be rooted in love, v17
4. Spiritual understanding, v18
5. To know the love of Christ, v19
6. To be filled with all the fullness of God, v18

Ephesians 1:17 -19 six things to pray for:
1. The spirit of wisdom, v17
2. The spirit of revelation, v17
3. Full enlightenment of truth v18
4. The hope of his calling v18
5. The riches of the glory of His inheritance in the saints, v18
6. The exceeding greatness of His power to those who believe, v19

POSITIONS OF PRAYER IN THE BIBLE
1. Kneeling
Solomon (1 Kings 8:54) Elijah (1 Kings 18:42) Ezra (Ezra 9:5) Daniel (Dan 6:10) Jesus (Luke 22:41) Stephen (Acts 9:40) Peter (Acts 7:60) Paul (Acts 20:36; Eph 3:14)
2. Standing
Mark 11:25 *And whenever you stand praying…* NKJV
Luke 18:11 *The Pharisee stood and prayed…* NKJV
1 Kings 8:22 *Then Solomon stood before the altar of the Lord in the presence of all the assembly of Israel, and spread out his hands toward heaven…* NKJV
3. Lifting hands
1 Tim 2:8 *I desire therefore that the men pray everywhere, lifting up holy hands.* NKJV
1 Kings 8:22 *Then Solomon stood before the altar of the Lord in the presence of all the assembly of Israel, and spread out his hands toward heaven;*

NKJV

Ps 141:2 *Let my prayer be set before You as incense, The lifting up of my hands as the evening sacrifice.* NKJV

4. Bowing

Gen 24:26 *Then the man bowed down his head and worshiped the Lord.* NKJV

Ex 4:31 *...then they bowed their heads and worshiped.* NKJV

Ex 34:8 *So Moses made haste and bowed his head toward the earth, and worshiped.* NKJV

5. On One's Face

Num 20:6 *...and they fell on their faces. And the glory of the Lord appeared to them.* NKJV

Josh 5:14 *And Joshua fell on his face to the earth and worshiped.* NKJV

Matt 26:39 *He went a little farther and fell on His face, and prayed.* NKJV

Deut 9:25 *Thus I prostrated myself before the Lord.* NKJV

6. Secret Prayer

Matt 6:6 *But thou, when thou prayest, enter into thy closet,* KJV

Acts 10:9 *Peter went up upon the housetop to pray about the sixth hour* KJV

Mark 1:35... *he went out, and departed into a solitary place, and there prayed.* KJV

Luke 5:16 *And he withdrew himself into the wilderness, and prayed.* KJV

Seven-fold way to answered prayer:
1. Pray to the Father (John 16:23)
2. In the name of Jesus (Jn 14:12-15)
3. By the Holy Spirit (Rom 8:26)
4. With full understanding of rights and privileges (1 Cor 14:14-15)
5. In harmony with the Word (In 15:7)
6. In faith, nothing doubting (James 1:6)
7. With praise for the answer r(Phil 4:6)

Pray for preachers: (Eph 6:19)
1. For inspired utterance
2. For boldness

3. For clarity

Matt 5:44 ...*pray for them which despitefully use you, and persecute you;* KJV

Matt 6:6 *But thou, when thou prayest, enter into thy closet, and when thou hast shut thy door, pray to thy Father which is in secret;* KJV

Matt 6:7 *But when ye pray, use not vain repetitions...* KJV

Luke 18:1 ...*men ought always to pray...* KJV

1 Thess 5:17 *Pray without ceasing.* KJV

EXAMPLES OF ANSWERED PRAYER
1. Jacob (Gen 35:3)
2. Moses (Ex 19:19; Ps 99:6)
3. Aaron (Ps 99:6)
4. Samuel (1 Sam 10:22; Ps 99:6)
5. David (1 Sam 23:4; 2 Sam 21:1)
6. Job (40:1)
7. Jesus (John 11:41-42)

Eph 6:18 (Ampl) *"Pray.....with all manner of prayer ...."*

INTERCESSORY
Ps 101:8 *Morning after morning I will root up all the wicked in the land, that I may eliminate all the evildoers from the city of the Lord.* AMP

Eph 6:18 *With all prayer and petition pray at all times in the Spirit, and with this in view, be on the alert with all perseverance and petition for all the saints...*

Ex 32:31 *"But now, if You will, forgive their sin — and if not, please blot me out from Your book which You have written!"*

Num 14:17 *But now, I pray, let the power of the Lord be great*

PETITION
Jude 20 ...*building yourselves up on your most holy faith, praying in the Holy Spirit.*

1 Sam 1:12-17 *Now it came about, as she continued praying before the Lord...13 As for Hannah, she was speaking in her heart, only her lips were moving, but her voice was not heard...15 I have poured out my soul before the Lord...17 "Go in peace; and may the God of Israel grant your petition that you have asked of Him."*

Acts 6:6 *...and after praying, they laid their hands on them.*
James 5:14 *Is anyone among you sick? Then he must call for the elders of the church and they are to pray over him, anointing him with oil in the name of the Lord...*

James 5:16-17 *The effective prayer of a righteous man can accomplish much.*

James 5:17-18 *...he prayed earnestly that it would not rain, and it did not rain on the earth for three years and six months. 18 Then he prayed again, and the sky poured rain and the earth produced its fruit*

PRIDE
A STUDY

Oba 3 *The pride of thine heart hath deceived thee... KJV*

Jer 17:9 *The heart is deceitful above all things, and desperately wicked: who can know it?* KJV

Prov 11:2 *When pride cometh, then cometh shame:* KJV

Prov 13:10 *Only by pride cometh contention:* KJV

1 Sam 17:28 *I know thy pride, and the naughtiness of thine hear...* KJV

Jer 48:29 *We have heard of the pride of Moab — he is very proud — Of his haughtiness, his pride, his arrogance and his self-exaltation.*

Jer 50:31-32 *"Behold, I am against you, O arrogant one,"...32 "The arrogant one will stumble and fall."*

2 Cor 11:17 *What I am saying, I am not saying as the Lord would, but as in foolishness, in this confidence of boasting...*

PRIDE IS WORLDLY
1 John 2:16 *For all that is in the world, the lust of the flesh and the lust of the eyes and the boastful pride of life, is not from the Father, but is from the world.*

Luke 14:11 *For everyone who exalts himself will be humbled...*

Prov 11:2 *When pride comes, then comes dishonor...*

PRIDE BRINGS A FALL
Prov 29:23 *A man's pride will bring him low, But a humble spirit will obtain honor.*

Prov 16:18 *Pride goes before destruction, And a haughty spirit before stumbling.*

Isa 2:12 ...*every one that is proud and lofty, and upon every one that is lifted up; and he shall be brought low:* KJV

Isa 2:17 *And the loftiness of man shall be bowed down, and the haughtiness of men shall be made low.* KJV

2 Sam 22:28 ...*thine eyes are upon the haughty, that thou mayest bring them down.*
KJV

1 Tim 3:6 ...lest being lifted up with pride he fall into the condemnation of the devil. KJV

Five examples of being brought low:
1. Lucifer (Isa 14:12; Rev 20:10)
2. Angels (2 Pet 2:4; Jude 6, 7)
3. Adam and Eve (Gen 3:5, 6
4. Nebuchadnezzar (Dan 4)
5. Belshazzar (Dan 5)

PRIDE KEEPS ONE FROM SEEKING GOD
Ps 10:4 *The wicked one in the pride of his countenance will not seek, inquire for, and yearn for God; all his thoughts are that there is no God.* AMP

PRIDE BRINGS STRIFE
Prov 28:25 *He who is of a greedy spirit stirs up strife, but he who puts his trust in the Lord shall be enriched and blessed.* AMP

Prov 13:10 *By pride and insolence comes only contention...* AMP

Four times pride brought contention:
1. Korah (Num 16)
2. Men of Ephraim (Judg 12:1-6)
3. Rehoboam (1 Kings 12)
4. The Apostles (Luke 22:24)

PRIDE IS CURED BY LOVE
1 Cor 13:4-7 *Love is patient, love is kind and is not jealous; love does not brag and is not arrogant, 5 does not act unbecomingly; it does not seek its own, is not*

provoked, does not take into account a wrong suffered, 6 does not rejoice in unrighteousness, but rejoices with the truth; 7 bears all things...

PRIDE BINDS

Ps 73:6 *Therefore pride is about their necks like a chain; violence covers them like a garment [like a long, luxurious robe].* AMP

PRIDE DEFILES

Mark 7:21-23 *For from within, out of the heart of men, proceed evil thoughts, adulteries, fornications, murders, 22 Thefts, covetousness, wickedness, deceit, lasciviousness, an evil eye, blasphemy, pride, foolishness: 23 All these evil things come from within, and defile the man.* KJV

PRIDE IS HATED BY GOD

Prov 8:13 *The fear of the Lord is to hate evil: pride, and arrogancy, and the evil way, and the froward mouth, do I hate.* KJV

God's hatred of pride is strong. It was a prideful, haughty spirit which brought Satan down.

GOD WILL PUNISH THE PROUD

Isa 13:11 *And I will punish the world for their evil, and the wicked for their iniquity;*
and I will cause the arrogancy of the proud to cease, and will lay low the haughtiness of the terrible. KJV

Isa 2:11 *The lofty looks of man shall be humbled, and the haughtiness of men shall be bowed down, and the Lord alone shall be exalted in that day.* KJV

PROMOTION

Ps 75:6-7 *For not from the east nor from the west nor from the south come promotion and lifting up. 7 But God is the Judge! He puts down one and lifts up another.* AMP

Ps 37:34 *Wait for and expect the Lord and keep and heed His way, and He will exalt you to inherit the land; [in the end] when the wicked are cut off, you shall see it.* AMP

Prov 4:8 *Prize Wisdom highly and exalt her, and she will exalt and promote you; she will bring you to honor when you embrace her.* AMP   skh

PROSPER
A STUDY

God wants His children to be blessed. There is a truthful saying, "a truly prosperous person, is one who has developed in God's Word." He or She, can be prosperous in every area of existence...in every area of the Scriptures. Because the Word is truth, my decision based on this Word is the right one because of the integrity of God.

Deut 29:9 *...keep the words of this covenant, and do them, that you may prosper in all that you do.* NKJV

GOD WILLS THAT WE PROSPER IN EVERY AREA OF LIFE
3 John 2-3 *Beloved, I pray that you may prosper in all things and be in health, just as your soul prospers.* NKJV

John 10:10 *The thief comes only in order to steal and kill and destroy. I came that they may have and enjoy life, and have it in abundance (to the full, till it overflows).* AMP

Isa 48:15 *... and his way will prosper.* NKJV

Zech 8:12 *For the seed shall be prosperous, The vine shall give its fruit, The ground shall give her increase, And the heavens shall give their dew...* NKJV

Deut 28:4-6 *"Blessed shall be the fruit of your body, the produce of your ground and the increase of your herds, the increase of your cattle and the offspring of your flocks. 5 "Blessed shall be your basket and your kneading bowl. 6 "Blessed shall you be when you come in, and blessed shall you be when you go out..."* NKJV

Neh 2:20 *... and said to them, "The God of heaven Himself will prosper us;* NKJV

Gen 24:56 *Do not hinder me, since the Lord has prospered my way;* NKJV

Gen 39:2 *The Lord was with Joseph, and he was a successful man;* NKJV

Prov 10:22 *The blessing of the Lord makes one rich...* NKJV

Deut 28:12 *The Lord will open to you His good treasure...* NKJV

Prov 15:6 *In the house of the righteous there is much treasure...* NKJV

Prov 3:9-10 *Honor the Lord from your wealth And from the first of all your produce; 10 So your barns will be filled with plenty And your vats will overflow with new wine.*

2 Cor 9:7-8 *Each one must do just as he has purposed in his heart, not grudgingly or under compulsion, for God loves a cheerful giver. 8 And God is able to make all grace abound to you, so that always having all sufficiency in everything, you may have an abundance for every good deed;*

Ps 112:3 *Wealth and riches will be in his house...* NKJV

Prov 8:21 *That I may cause those who love me to inherit wealth, That I may fill their treasuries.* NKJV

GOD PROSPERS US AS WE KEEP HIS WORD

Deut 29:9 *Therefore keep the words of this covenant, and do them, that you may prosper in all that you do.* NKJV

Ps 1:2-3 *But his delight is in the law of the Lord, And in His law he meditates day and night. 3 He shall be like a tree Planted by the rivers of water, That brings forth its fruit in its season, Whose leaf also shall not wither; And whatever he does shall prosper.* NKJV

Josh 1:8 *This Book of the Law shall not depart from your mouth, but you shall meditate in it day and night, that you may observe to do according to all that is written in it. For then you will make your way prosperous, and then you will have good success.* NKJV

Isa 55:11 *So shall My word be that goes forth from My mouth; It shall not return to Me void, But it shall accomplish what I please, And it shall prosper in the thing for which I sent it.* NKJV

John 15:6-8 *If you abide in Me, and My words abide in you, you will ask what you desire, and it shall be done for you.* NKJV

GOD PROSPERS US AS WE SEEK THE LORD
2 Chron 26:5 ... *as long as he sought the Lord, God made him prosper.* NKJV

Ps 107:9 *For He has satisfied the thirsty soul, And the hungry soul He has filled with what is good.*

PRAY TO PROSPER
Neh 1:11 *"O Lord, I beseech You, may Your ear be attentive to the prayer of Your servant and the prayer of Your servants who delight to revere Your name, and make Your servant successful today and grant him compassion before this man."*

THE WORLDLY CAN PROSPER ALSO
Neh 1:11 *"O Lord, I beseech You, may Your ear be attentive to the prayer of Your servant and the prayer of Your servants who delight to revere Your name, and make Your servant successful today and grant him compassion before this man."*

Ps 37:35 *I have seen the wicked in great power...* NKJV

Ps 73:3 *For I was envious of the boastful, When I saw the prosperity of the wicked.* NKJV

Ps 73:12 *Behold, these are the ungodly, Who are always at ease; They increase in riches.* NKJV

Prov 1:32 *For the waywardness of the naive will kill them, And the complacency of fools will destroy them.*

BE AWARE OF TWO TEMPTATIONS OF PROSPERITY
1. Pride, self-edification
Deut 8:14 *...your heart will become proud and you will forget the Lord your God who brought you out from the land of Egypt, out of the house of slavery.*

2. Tendency to forget God as the source of every blessing

Deut 8:17-18 *"Otherwise, you may say in your heart, 'My power and the strength of my hand made me this wealth.' 18 "But you shall remember the Lord your God, for it is He who is giving you power to make wealth..."*

PROTECTION OR SAFETY

(See Safety, separate topic)

Ps 91

He who dwells in the secret place of the Most High Shall abide under the shadow of the Almighty. 2 I will say of the Lord, "He is my refuge and my fortress; My God, in Him I will trust."

3 Surely He shall deliver you from the snare of the fowler And from the perilous pestilence. 4 He shall cover you with His feathers, And under His wings you shall take refuge; His truth shall be your shield and buckler. 5 You shall not be afraid of the terror by night, Nor of the arrow that flies by day, 6 Nor of the pestilence that walks in darkness, Nor of the destruction that lays waste at noonday.

7 A thousand may fall at your side, And ten thousand at your right hand; But it shall not come near you. 8 Only with your eyes shall you look, And see the reward of the wicked.

9 Because you have made the Lord, who is my refuge, Even the Most High, your dwelling place, 10 No evil shall befall you, Nor shall any plague come near your dwelling; 11 For He shall give His angels charge over you, To keep you in all your ways. 12 In their hands they shall bear you up, Lest you dash your foot against a stone. 13 You shall tread upon the lion and the cobra, The young lion and the serpent you shall trample underfoot.

14 "Because he has set his love upon Me, therefore I will deliver him; I will set him on high, because he has known My name. 15 He shall call upon Me, and I will answer him; I will be with him in trouble; I will deliver him and honor him. 16 With long life I will satisfy him, And show him My salvation." NKJV

PROTECTION NIGHT OR DAY, AND WHILE TRAVELING

Isa 14:30 *...the needy will lie down in safety;* NKJV

Prov 3:23-26 *Then you will walk safely in your way, And your foot will not stumble. 24 When you lie down, you will not be afraid; Yes, you will lie down and your sleep will be sweet. 25 Do not be afraid of sudden terror, Nor of trouble from the wicked when it comes; 26 For the Lord will be your confidence, And will keep your foot from being caught.* NKJV

Ps 91:5 *You shall not be afraid of the terror by night, Nor of the arrow that flies by Day...* NKJV

Ps 33:17-20 *A horse is a vain hope for safety; Neither shall it deliver any by its great strength. 18 Behold, the eye of the Lord is on those who fear Him, On those who hope in His mercy, 19 To deliver their soul from death, And to keep them alive in famine. 20 Our soul waits for the Lord; He is our help and our shield.* NKJV

Ps 121:6-7 *The sun shall not strike you by day, Nor the moon by night. 7 The Lord shall preserve you...* NKJV

Deut 31:8 *It is the Lord Who goes before you; He will [march] with you; He will not fail you or let you go or forsake you; [let there be no cowardice or flinching, but] fear not, neither become broken.* AMP

GOD IS OUR SAFETY FOR OUR FAMILIES

Isa 14:30 *And the needy will lie down in safety;* NKJV

Prov 3:23-26 *Then you will walk safely in your way, And your foot will not stumble. 24 When you lie down, you will not be afraid; Yes, you will lie down and your sleep will be sweet. 25 Do not be afraid of sudden terror, Nor of trouble from the wicked when it comes; 26 For the Lord will be your confidence, And will keep your foot from being caught.* NKJV

Prov 29:25 *...whoever trusts in the Lord shall be safe.* NKJV

Ps 78:53 *And He led them on safely, so that they did not fear;* NKJV

Ps 4:8 *...O Lord, make me dwell in safety.* NKJV

Ps 121:3-7 *He will not allow your foot to slip or to be moved; He Who keeps you will not slumber. [1 Sam 2:9; Ps 127:1; Prov 3:23,26; Isa 27:3.] 5 The Lord is your keeper; the Lord is your shade on your right hand [the side not carrying a shield]. [Isa 25:4.] 6 The sun shall not smite you by day, nor the moon by night. [Ps 91:5; Isa 49:10; Rev 7:16.] 7 The Lord will keep you from all evil; He will keep your life.* AMP

PROTECTION IS IN THE NAME OF THE LORD
Prov 18:10 *The name of the Lord is a strong tower; The righteous runs into it and is safe.*

John 16:24 *Until now you have asked for nothing in My name; ask and you will receive, so that your joy may be made full.*

Ps 9:9-10 *The Lord also will be a stronghold for the oppressed, A stronghold in times of trouble; 10 And those who know Your name will put their trust in You, For You, O Lord, have not forsaken those who seek You.*

GOD IS OUR SAFETY IN BATTLES
Prov 21:31 *The horse is prepared for the day of battle, But victory belongs to the Lord.*

Ps 91:7 *A thousand may fall at your side And ten thousand at your right hand, But it shall not approach you.*

2 Chron 20:22 *When they began singing and praising, the Lord set ambushes against the sons of Ammon, Moab and Mount Seir, who had come against Judah; so they were routed.*

IN MAKING DECISIONS
Prov 11:14 *Where there is no guidance the people fall, But in abundance of counselors there is victory.*

REDEEMED

Ex 15:13 *In Your lovingkindness You have led the people whom You have redeemed;*

Isa 43:1 *Do not fear, for I have redeemed you;*

Isa 43:14 *...the Lord your Redeemer...*

Isa 48:20 *The Lord has redeemed His servant Jacob.*

Prov 23:11 *Redeemer is strong; He will plead their case against you.*

Mark 10:45 *For even the Son of Man did not come to be served, but to serve, and to give His life a ransom for many.*

Eph 1:7 *...In Him we have redemption*

1 Cor 6:20 *For you have been bought with a price: therefore glorify God in your body.*

Heb 9:15 *...those who have been called may receive the promise of the eternal inheritance.*

Eph 4:30 *...you were sealed for the day of redemption.*

REST (also see SLEEP)

Josh 1:13-14 *'The Lord your God gives you rest and will give you this land.'*

Heb 4:1 *Therefore, let us fear if, while a promise remains of entering His rest, any one of you may seem to have come short of it.*

Matt 11:28 *Come to Me, all who are weary and heavy-laden, and I will give you rest.*

1 Peter 5:7-8 *...casting all your anxiety on Him, because He cares for you.*

Ps 55:22 *Cast your burden upon the Lord and He will sustain you; He will never allow the righteous to be shaken.*

RICHES

A STUDY

GOD'S ATTITUDE TOWARD RICHES IN THE OLD TESTAMENT

Gen 13:2 *Now Abram was very rich in livestock, in silver and in gold...*

1 Chron 29:12 *Both riches and honor come from You...*

2 Chron 17:5-6 *... and he had great riches and honor.*

Deut 28:12-13 *The Lord will open for you His good storehouse, the heavens, to give rain to your land in its season and to bless all the work of your hand; and you shall lend to many nations, but you shall not borrow.*

2 Chron 32:27-29 *Now Hezekiah had immense riches and honor; and he made for himself treasuries for silver, gold, precious stones, spices, shields and all kinds of valuable articles, 28 storehouses also for the produce of grain, wine and oil, pens for all kinds of cattle and sheepfolds for the flocks. 29 He made cities for himself and acquired flocks and herds in abundance, for God had given him very great wealth.*

Gen 26:14 *...he had possessions of flocks and herds and a great household, so that the Philistines envied him.*

Deut 8:12-14 *...when you have eaten and are satisfied, and have built good houses and lived in them, 13 and when your herds and your flocks multiply, and your silver and gold multiply, and all that you have multiplies...*

Gen 30:43 *So the man became exceedingly prosperous, and had large flocks and female and male servants and camels and donkeys.*

GOD'S ATTITUDE TOWARD RICHES IN THE NEW TESTAMENT

Phil 4:19-20 *...my God will supply all your needs according to His riches in glory in Christ Jesus.*

Matt 6:33 *...seek first His kingdom and His righteousness, and all these things will be added to you.*

2 Peter 1:3 *His divine power has granted to us everything pertaining to life and Godliness.*

1 Cor 3:21 *For all things are yours.* NKJV

Matt 27:57 *...a rich man from Arimathea, named Joseph...* NKJV

3 John 2 *Beloved, I pray that you may prosper in all things...* NKJV

Luke 4:18 *"The Spirit of the Lord is upon Me, Because He has anointed Me To preach the gospel to the poor;"* NKJV

2 Cor 8:9 *He became poor, that you through His poverty might become rich.* NKJV

1 Tim 6:17 *Command those who are rich in this present age not to be haughty.* NKJV

Deut 8:18 *And you shall remember the Lord your God, for it is* He who gives you power to get wealth... NKJV

Ps 23:1 *The Lord is my shepherd, I shall not want.*

Prov 10:22 *It is the blessing of the Lord that makes rich...*

Ps 104:24 *...the earth is full of Your riches.* AMP

RICHES ARE FOR THE UPRIGHT
Ps 84:11 *No good thing does He withhold from those who walk uprightly.*

Prov 22:4 *The reward of humility and the fear of the Lord Are riches, honor and life.*

Prov 8:21 *To endow those who love me with wealth, That I may fill their treasuries.*

Prov 15:6 *Great wealth is in the house of the righteous,*

Ps 21:2-3 *You have given him his heart's desire, And You have not withheld the request of his lips. Selah. 3 For You meet him with the blessings of good things;*

Ps 34:8-9 *8 O taste and see that the Lord is good; How blessed is the man who takes refuge in Him! 9 O fear the Lord, you His saints; For to those who fear Him there is no want.*

Ps 112:1-3 *How blessed is the man who fears the Lord, Who greatly delights in His commandments. 2 His descendants will be mighty on earth; The generation of the upright will be blessed. 3 Wealth and riches are in his house,*

Isa 1:19 *If you consent and obey, You will eat the best of the land;*

RICHES GATHERED BY THE WORLD FOR BELIEVERS
Prov 13:22 *...the wealth of the sinner is stored up for the righteous.*

Prov 28:8 *He who increases his wealth by interest and usury Gathers it for him who is gracious to the poor.*

Job 27:16-17 *Though he piles up silver like dust And prepares garments as plentiful as the clay, 17 He may prepare it, but the just will wear it And the innocent will divide the silver.*

Ps 105:44 *He gave them also the lands of the nations, That they might take possession of the fruit of the peoples' labor...*

Eccl 2:26 *...to the sinner He gives the work of gathering and heaping up, that he may give to one who pleases God.* AMP

Deut 6:10 *...to give you, with great and goodly cities which you did not build,* AMP

Isa 60:11 *...that men may bring to you the wealth of the nations...*

Ps 111:5-6 *He hath given meat unto them that fear him: he will ever be mindful of his covenant. 6 He hath shewed his people the power of his works, that he may give them the heritage of the heathen.* KJV

RICHES COME BY THE WORD OF GOD

Prov 3:16 *Long life is in her right hand; In her left hand are riches and honor.*
Prov 8:18 *Riches and honor are with me, Enduring wealth and righteousness.*

Ps 112:1-3 *How blessed is the man who fears the Lord, Who greatly delights in His commandments. 2 His descendants will be mighty on earth; The generation of the upright will be blessed. 3 Wealth and riches are in his house...*

Deut 28:2-5 *All these blessings will come upon you and overtake you if you obey the Lord your God: 3 "Blessed shall you be in the city, and blessed shall you be in the country...5 "Blessed shall be your basket and your kneading bowl.*

DO NOT LET FINANCES BECOME YOUR GOD
Luke 1:53 *He has filled the hungry with good things, And the rich He has sent away empty.* NKJV

Luke 6:24 *But woe to you who are rich, for you are receiving your comfort in full...*

1 Tim 6:9-10 *But those who want to get rich fall into temptation and a snare and many foolish and harmful desires which plunge men into ruin and destruction. 10 For the love of money is a root of all sorts of evil, and some by longing for it have wandered away from the faith and pierced themselves with many griefs.*

Lavishness in not God's norm...where your treasure is...there is your heart.

Prov 28:20 *A faithful man will abound with blessings, But he who makes haste to be rich will not go unpunished.*

Mark 10:24 *...how hard it is for those who trust in riches to enter the kingdom of God.* NKJV

Ps 62:10 *If riches increase, Do not set your heart on them.* NKJV

Luke 12:15 *Then He said to them, "Beware, and be on your guard against every form of greed; for not even when one has an abundance does his life consist of his possessions."*

Matt 6:19-21 *Do not store up for yourselves treasures on earth, where moth and rust destroy, and where thieves break in and steal. 20 "But store up for yourselves treasures in heaven, where neither moth nor rust destroys, and where thieves do not break in or steal; 21 for where your treasure is, there your heart will be also.*

TIMES OF FAMINE AND PERSECUTION

Ps 37:19 *...in the days of famine they will have abundance.*

Ps 33:19 *...keep them alive in famine.*

Gen 26:1-3 *Now there was a famine in the land, besides the previous famine that had occurred in the days of Abraham. So Isaac went to Gerar, to Abimelech king of the Philistines. 2 The Lord appeared to him and said, "Do not go down to Egypt; stay in the land of which I shall tell you. 3 "Sojourn in this land and I will be with you and bless you, for to you and to your descendants I will give all these lands, and I will establish the oath which I swore to your father Abraham.*

Ps 66:12 *We went through fire and through water, Yet You brought us out into a place of abundance.*

Love of money=Destruction of faith

(James 2:5; Prov 28:20; 1 Tim 6:10; Mark 10:24; Prov 1:28; Ps 62:10).

RIGHTEOUSNESS

Isa 53:11 *By His knowledge the Righteous One, My Servant, will justify the many, As He will bear their iniquities.*

2 Cor 5:21 *He made Him who knew no sin to be sin on our behalf, so that we might become the righteousness of God in Him.*

Isa 54:14 *In righteousness you will be established:* NIV

2 Tim 2:22 *...pursue righteousness...*

1 Cor 1:30-31 *But of Him you are in Christ Jesus, who became for us wisdom from God — and righteousness and sanctification and redemption.* NKJV

Matt 5:6 *Blessed are those who hunger and thirst for righteousness...* NKJV

Matt 6:33 *...seek first His kingdom and His righteousness...*

Rom 1:16-17 *For I am not ashamed of the gospel, for it is the power of God for salvation to everyone who believes, to the Jew first and also to the Greek. 17 For in it the righteousness of God is revealed from faith to faith; as it is written, "BUT THE RIGHTEOUS man SHALL LIVE BY FAITH."*

Rom 10:10 *...for with the heart a person believes, resulting in righteousness...*

Eph 4:23-24 *...be renewed in the spirit of your mind, 24 and that you put on the new man which was created according to God, in true righteousness and holiness.* NKJV

Rom 5:16-17 *For if by the transgression of the one, death reigned through the one, much more those who receive the abundance of grace and of the gift of righteousness will reign in life through the One, Jesus Christ.*

1 Cor 15:34 *Awake to righteousness, and do not sin;* NKJV

SAFETY

Prov 29:25 *The fear of man brings a snare, But he who trusts in the Lord will be exalted.*

1 John 5:4 *For whatever is born of God overcomes the world; and this is the victory that has overcome the world — our faith.*

1 John 4:4 *You are from God, little children, and have overcome them; because greater is He who is in you than he who is in the world.*

John 14:27 *Peace I leave with you; My peace I give to you;*

1 John 5:1 *This is the confidence which we have before Him, that, if we ask anything according to His will, He hears us.*

Luke 10:19 *Behold, I have given you authority to tread on serpents and scorpions, and over all the power of the enemy, and nothing will injure you.*

Ps 12:5 *I will arise," says the Lord; "I will set him in the safety for which he longs."*

Ps 36:5 *Your lovingkindness, O Lord, extends to the heavens, Your faithfulness reaches to the skies.*

Isa 14:30 *Those who are most helpless will eat, And the needy will lie down in security;*

Prov 3:23-25 *Then you will walk in your way securely And your foot will not stumble. 24 When you lie down, you will not be afraid; When you lie down, your sleep will be sweet. 25 Do not be afraid of sudden fear...*

Prov 29:25 *The fear of man brings a snare, But he who trusts in the Lord will be exalted.*

Heb 13:5-6 *He Himself has said, "I WILL NEVER DESERT YOU, NOR WILL I EVER FORSAKE YOU," 6 so that we confidently say, "THE LORD IS MY HELPER, I WILL NOT BE AFRAID. WHAT WILL MAN DO TO ME?"*

Ps 145:20 *The Lord keeps all who love Him...*

Ps 27:1 *The Lord is my light and my salvation; Whom shall I fear? The Lord is the defense of my life; Whom shall I dread?*

Prov 12:21 *No harm befalls the righteous...*

Ps 68:20-21 *God is to us a God of deliverances; And to God the Lord belong escapes from death. 21 Surely God will shatter the head of His enemies...*

Salvation

A STUDY

SIX SCRIPTURAL STEPS TO SALVATION

1. Acknowledge: Rom 3:23 *for all have sinned and fall short of the glory of God.* NKJV

2. Repent: Luke 18:11 *'God, be merciful to me, the sinner!'*

3. Confess: Rom 10:9-10 *if you confess with your mouth Jesus as Lord, and believe in your heart that God raised Him from the dead, you will be saved.*

4. Forsake: Isa 55:7 *Let the wicked forsake his way And the unrighteous man his thoughts; And let him return to the Lord, And He will have compassion on him.*

5. Believe: John 3:16 *For God so loved the world, that He gave His only begotten Son, that whoever believes in Him shall not perish, but have eternal life.*

6. Receive: John 1:12 *But as many as received Him, to them He gave the right to become children of God.*

ABC's OF SALVATION

All have sinned and come short of the glory of God (Rom 3:23); **A**dmit it! *(*1 Jn 3:16).

Believe on the Lord Jesus Christ and you will be saved (John 3:16).

Call upon the name of the Lord and you will be saved (Rom 10:13); *Confess your sins, He is faithful and just to forgive you* (1 John 1:19).

ADDITIONAL DETAILS ON SALVATION

ALL HAVE SINNED

Rom 3:23 *For all have sinned... KJV*

Rom 3:10 *There is none righteous, no, not one: KJV*

HE DESIRES TO SAVE ANYONE

John 6:37 *...the one who comes to Me I will certainly not cast out.*

1 Tim 2:4-5 *...who desires all men to be saved and to come to the knowledge of the truth.*

2 Peter 3:9 *The Lord is not slow about His promise, as some count slowness, but is patient toward you, not wishing for any to perish but for all to come to repentance.*

Luke 9:56 *"...for the Son of Man did not come to destroy men's lives, but to save them."*

Luke 19:11 *"For the Son of Man has come to seek and to save that which was lost."*

HE MADE A WAY FOR YOU TO BE SAVED

Matt 1:21 *"She will bear a Son; and you shall call His name Jesus, for He will save His people from their sins."*

John 3:16 *For God so loved the world, that He gave His only begotten Son, that whoever believes in Him shall not perish, but have eternal life.*

John 11:25 *Jesus said to her, "I am the resurrection and the life; he who believes in Me will live..."*

John 14:6 *I am the way, and the truth, and the life;*

Rom 10:13 *"WHOEVER WILL CALL ON THE NAME OF THE LORD WILL BE SAVED."*

Acts 16:31 *They said, "Believe in the Lord Jesus, and you will be saved..."*

John 3:36 *He who believes in the Son has eternal life.*

John 1:12 *But as many as received Him, to them He gave the right to become children of God...*

John 10:9 *I am the door; if anyone enters through Me, he will be saved...*

John 3:3 *Jesus answered and said to him, "Truly, truly, I say to you, unless one is born again he cannot see the kingdom of God."*
John 6:37 *...the one who comes to Me I will certainly not cast out.*

SALVATION IS FREE
Rom 6:23 *...the free gift of God is eternal life in Christ Jesus our Lord.*

Eph 2:8 *For by grace you have been saved through faith; and that not of yourselves, it is the gift of God...*

Rom 10:9 *...if you confess with your mouth Jesus as Lord, and believe in your heart that God raised Him from the dead, you will be saved;*

Acts 4:12 *"And there is salvation in no one else; for there is no other name under heaven that has been given among men by which we must be saved."*

Rev 3:20 *Behold, I stand at the door and knock; if anyone hears My voice and opens the door, I will come in to him...*

WHAT HAPPENS AT SALVATION?
Rom 8:11 *His Spirit who dwells in you.*

1 John 1:7 *...the blood of Jesus His Son cleanses us from all sin.*

John 1:12 *He gave the right to become children of God...*

John 1:12 *He gave the right to become children of God...*

Acts 3:19 *...repent and return, so that your sins may be wiped away...*

Isa 43:25 *I, even I, am the one who wipes out your transgressions...*

Heb 8:12 *"I WILL REMEMBER THEIR SINS NO MORE."*

SATAN
A DETAILED STUDY

While not an enjoyable subject to study, it is vital to our Christian walk that we have a thorough understanding of Satan. "Know thy enemy." So, I'm placing before you, certain facts about him. The Scriptures are explicit; they inform us as much about Satan as about God. They inform us as to who he was and who he is today, how he became what he is, and how he gained dominion over the human race. Also, we are told of his nature and character, and best of all, his end.

ORIGIN

Ps 148:2-5 *...all His angels; 5 For He commanded and they were created.*

Col 1:16 *For it was in Him that all things were created, in heaven and on earth, things seen and things unseen, whether thrones, dominions, rulers, or authorities; all things were created...* AMP

Ezek 28:15 *You were blameless in your ways From the day you were created Until unrighteousness was found in you.*

Ezekiel 28 describes him:
12 "You had the seal of perfection,
Full of wisdom and perfect in beauty.
13 "You were in Eden, the garden of God;
Every precious stone was your covering:
The ruby, the topaz and the diamond;
The beryl, the onyx and the jasper;
The lapis lazuli, the turquoise and the emerald;
And the gold, the workmanship of your settings and sockets,
Was in you.
On the day that you were created
They were prepared.
14 "You were the anointed cherub who covers,
And I placed you there.
You were on the holy mountain of God;
You walked in the midst of the stones of fire.

15 "You were blameless in your ways
From the day you were created
Until unrighteousness was found in you.
16 "By the abundance of your trade
You were internally filled with violence,
And you sinned;

(Satan was created full of great wisdom and beauty. Satan was connected with the very throne of God. He, being a musician, led the heavenly musicians and chorus in the worship of God. He was able to walk up and down in the very presence of the Eternal God, and was perfect. *But something happened...*)

17 "Your heart was lifted up because of your beauty;
You corrupted your wisdom by reason of your splendor.

(This heavenly being, who held a place of authority and glory and honor before God, was cast out of heaven along with 1/3 of the angels. A special burning lake was created to be their eternal home. **In** his fall from heaven, Satan lost none of his ability or brilliancy, and none of this wisdom or love of music; it simply became corrupted.)

Later it was recorded in Luke 10:18 that Jesus said *And He said to them, "I was watching Satan fall from heaven like lightning..."*

Isaiah records (14:13-14) that Satan said: *'I will ascend to heaven; I will raise my throne above the stars of God, And I will sit on the mount of assembly In the recesses of the north. 14 'I will ascend above the heights of the clouds; I will make myself like the Most High.'*

And it's recorded in vv 12 *How you have fallen from heaven, O star of the morning, son of the dawn! You have been cut down to the earth, You who have weakened the nations!*

Ezek 28:17 records *I will cast thee to the ground.* KJV

SATAN'S LEGAL DOMNION

One of the bitterest facts that humanity and Heaven have to face is that Satan has a legal right to rule over the human race!

1. God gave to Adam the dominion and authority to rule. This included Satan and all the works of God's hands. Man ruled not only Satan but also the angelic beings. He was next to God in authority.

2. Adam turned that vast Kingdom rule over to the hands of Satan by disobedience to God. It was a legal transference, recognized by God. The only was to meet this issue was to send His Son down out of Heaven to suffer the penalty of Adam's transgression. Thus, God began the Plan of Redemption.

3. Throughout the Scriptures, God and His angels treat Satan with a recognition of his legal dominion. God could not put him out of business and drive him off the earth.

> Jude 9-10 *But Michael the archangel, when he disputed with the devil and argued about the body of Moses, did not dare pronounce against him a railing judgment, but said, "The Lord rebuke you!"*

> Zech 3:1-2 *Then he showed me Joshua the high priest standing before the angel of the Lord, and Satan standing at his right hand to accuse him. 2 The Lord said to Satan, "The Lord rebuke you, Satan!*

> Satan was greater than any angelic being; even God's angel dared not rebuke him, rather shows him a peculiar respect and honor, reflecting the legal place that Satan had.

1 John 5:19-20 *...the whole world lies in the power of the evil one.*

4. Jesus did not dispute Satan's claim of legal dominion over the earth when they met in the wilderness. Satan had legal rights that both Jesus and God recognized. Look at the record in Luke 4:6-8 *the devil said to Him, "I will give You all this domain and its glory; for it has been handed over to me, and I give it to whomever I wish. 7 "Therefore if You worship before me, it shall all be Yours."*

It was not a lie. Satan had legal dominion. He had 1/3 of the angels and many Old Testament persons in his prison, now he tried to deceive the very Son of God. If he had been successful, Satan would have ruled the world for eternity.

HIS LEGAL DOMINION INCLUDES GREAT POWER

Luke 12:5-6 ...*fear the One who, after He has killed, has authority to cast into hell; yes, I tell you, fear Him!*

Heb 2:14-15 ...*him who had the power of death, that is, the devil.*

SATAN'S PLAN AND WORK

John 10:10 *The thief comes only to steal and kill and destroy...*

His chief desire and design is to steal, kill and destroy the human race and thereby bring sorrow to the heart of the Father God. He is the king or ruling angel of hell and its dark forces. He knows of his end and eternal abode; will seek who he may devour.

According to the Scriptures, he has the power of death, the power to bring plagues upon humanity, and the power to cause storms and unnatural fires.

- He is the deceiver of all men (2 Cor 11:14; Rev 12:9)
- He causes sickness, disease (Luke 14:16; Acts 10:38)
- Tempts men (Mark 1:13; 1 Cor 7:5)
- Provokes to sin (1 Chr 21:1)
- Transforms into an angel of light (2 Cor 11:14)
- Enters unions against God (Luke 22:3; John 13:2)
- Hinders the gospel (Acts 13:10; 1 Thess 2:18)
- Steals the Word of God (Matt 13:19; Luke 8:12)
- Works miracles (2 Thess 2:9)
- Hinders answers to prayer (Dan 10:12-21)
- Sets snares for men to fall into sin (1 Tim 3:7; 2 Tim 2:26)
- Blinds men to the gospel (2 Cor 4:4)
- Causes double mindedness (James 1:5-9)
- Causes doubt and unbelief (Gen 3:4-5; Rom 14:23)
- Causes delay and compromise (Acts 24:25; 26:28)
- Causes division and strife (1 Cor 3:1-3; 1 Pet 5:8)

Satan's work in a large part, is to counterfeit the doctrines and experiences from God in order to deceive the Christian (2 Cor 11:14-15; Eph 6:10-18; 1 Tim 4:1-7).

We are commanded to prove and test all doctrines and experiences to see if they are of God or Satan (1 Cor 2:12-16; Phil 1:9-10; 1 Thess 5:21-22).

It is certain that every religion, doctrine, and experience among man cannot be of Cod. Judge them by the Word of Cod. 2 Tim 2:15 *Study and be eager and do your utmost to present yourself to God approved (tested by trial), a workman who has no cause to be ashamed, correctly analyzing and accurately dividing [rightly handling and skillfully teaching] the Word of Truth.* AMP

Any doctrine that denies or causes doubt concerning anything taught in Scripture is from Satan (1 Tim 4:1-8).

NAMES/DESCRIPTIONS/SYMBOLS OF SATAN

The names, descriptions, and symbols associated with Satan, reveal his character.

1. *Devil,* meaning 'Accuser, Defamer, Slanderer' (1 Pet 5:8; Matt 4:1-11; Eph 6:11).
2. *Adversary (1* Pet 5:8; 1 Tim 5:14).
3. *Satan* (Rev 12:9; Lk 10:18;11:18).
4. *Belial* (worthlessness, wickedness (2 Cor 6:15; Deut 13;13).
5. *Lucifer* (Isa 14:12-14).
6. *Dragon* (Rev 12:3-17; 13:2-11; 20:2).
7. *Enemy* (Matt 13:39; Lk 10:19).
8. *Tempter* (Matt 4:3; 1 Thess 3:5).
9. *Wicked One* (Matt 13:19; 1 John 5:18).
10. *Beelzebub* (god of flies, dung god, prince of demons (Matt 10:25).
11. *God of this world* (2 Cor 4:4.
12. *Prince of this world* (John 12:31.
13. *Accuser of the Brethren* (Rev 12:10).
14. *Prince of the power of the air* (Eph 2:1-3; 6:12).
15. *The Anointed Cherub* (Ezek 28:11,17).
16. *King over all children of pride* (Job 41:34).
17. *Angel of Light* (2 Cor 11:14).
18. *Prince of Devils* (Matt 12:24).
19. *The Thief* (John 10:10).
20. *Leviathan* (crooked serpent) (Job 41:1; Isa 27:1).
21. *Power of Darkness* (Col 1:13).
22. Murderer and Liar (John 8:44).

SYMBOLS USED OF SATAN

1. Serpent, meaning "fascinator" (2 Cor 11:3; Gen 3:15; Luke 10:19).
2. Sea Monster (crocodile, whale, reptile, snake (Job 41:1; Isa 27:1).
3. Great red dragon (Rev 12:13; 16:13; 20:2).

4. Angel of light (2 Cor 11:14).
5. Roaring Lion (1 Pet 5:8; Ps 91:3).
6. Fowls (Matt 13:4, 19).
7. Scorpions (Luke 10:19.
8. Wolf (John 10:12).
9. Adder (Ps 91:14).

Think on all these names and symbols...what a picture of evil described. No wonder we hate this "force."

DESCRIBED AS A PERSON

He is not some evil principle, a disease germ, a being with hoofs, horns, tail, and shoes, holding a pitchfork and presiding over a place of fire and realm of the dead. This portrayal of Satan originated during the middle ages to resist evil by making mockery of him with ludicrous descriptions.

1. Jesus dealt with Satan as with a person (Matt 4:1-11; Luke 4:1-13).
2. Jesus waged war on Satan as on a person (Luke 13:16; 1 John 3:8; Acts 10:38).
3. Jesus taught that Satan was as a real person (Luke 10:18; Rev 12:7-12).
4. The apostles fought with Satan as with a real person (Eph 6:10-18; 1 Thess 2:18; 1 Pet 5:8-9).
5. Personal singular pronouns are used of Satan (Matt 4:7-11; 12:26; Luke 11:18).
6. Personal statements are made to him (14:12-14; Ezek 28:11-17; Job 1:6-12, 2:1-
   7; Matt 4:1-10; Jude 9).
7. Personal conversation is carried on with him (Matt 4:1-10; Job 1:6-12; Jude 9).
8. Personal descriptions are given of him (Isa 14:12-14; Ezek 28:11-17).
9. He has been seen with a body (1 Chr 21:1; Ps 109:6; Zech 3:1-2; Matt 4:1-11).
10. He has a *heart* (Isa 14:12-14), *speech* (Job 1:6-12; Matt 4:1-1), *power* (Job 1:6-22; Acts 10:38; 2 Thess 2:8-12) *lusts* (John 8:44; Eph 2:1-3), knowledge (job 1:6-12; Matt 4:1-11).
11. He goes from place to place in a body like anyone else (Job 12:8-12; Matt 4:1-11; Mark 4:15).
12. He has a kingdom (Mark 32:22-26).
13. His realm is divided into organized groups (Dan 10:12; Matt 12:24-30; Eph 6: 10-12).
14. His subjects are fallen angels, fallen men, and demons of various kinds, (Matt Matt 25:41; Rev 12:7-12; John 8:44; 1 John 3:8-10; James 2:19).

SIX THINGS A *SINGLE* ANGEL DOES TO SATAN

1. Lays hold on him
2. Binds him with a literal chain
3. Casts him into the abyss
4. Shuts him in prison
5. Sets a seal upon him for 1000 years
6. Looses him for a little season (perhaps 3 ½ years, as the same identified 'short time' of Rev 12:12; 17:10, following the 1000 years.

HIS LAST DAYS AND HIS END

Gen 3:15 PREDICTS IT...*And I will put enmity Between you and the woman, And between your seed and her seed* (Jesus); *He shall bruise you on the head,* (Christ shall utterly crush and eternally defeat Satan with a fatal blow to the head*) And you shall bruise him on the heel"* (Satan will inflict only temporary suffering on Jesus).

Rev 20:10 FULFILLS IT...*And the devil who deceived them was thrown into the lake of fire and brimstone, where the beast and the false prophet are also; and they will be tormented day and night forever and ever.*

A SUMMARY OF SATAN'S LAST DAYS

1. When the 1000 years are ended, it will be a time for the segregation and destruction of all rebels, including Satan, and the renovation of the heavens and the earth by fire, which will result in the New Heaven and New Earth (2 Pet 3:10-13; Rev 21:1-22:5).

2. Satan, his angels and demons will be loosed from the abyss (Isa 4:20 Rev 20:7).

3. Satan and his hosts will go through out the earth to deceive the nations who have not wanted the reign of Christ, and who in their hearts have longed for an opportunity to get rid of rigid laws that have suppressed their lusts. (Rev 20:8; Eph 2:1-3).

4. The rebels will mobilize in the land of God and Magog, North of Palestine and ascend upon Jerusalem (Rev. 20:8).

5. The rebels from all parts of the earth will surround the camp of the saints and the capital, Jerusalem (Rev. 20:9).

6. Fire will come down from God out of heaven and devour every rebel (Rev 20:9; 2 Pet 3:10-13).

7. The devil will be taken, judged, and cast into the lake of fire forever (Rev 20:10).

OUR RESPONSIBILITIES NOW
1. Put on the whole armor of God (Eph 6:11-18).
2. Know Satan's devices (2 Cor 2:11).
3. Give him no place in your life (Eph 4:27).
4. Resist him (James 4:7; 1 Pet 5:8-9).
5. Overcome him by the Word of God (Matt 4:11; 1 John 2:14).
6. Overcome him by the blood of the lamb (Rev 12:11).

QUICK CAPSULE/SUMMARY OF SATAN
1. He was an angel of light and led the worship in Heaven.
2. He was "The anointed cherub that covered," and stood near the Throne of God.
3. He fell by trying to take the Throne from God.
4. He was perfect in beauty and wisdom.
5. He lost none of his wisdom and love for music.
6. His nature was not changed by his fall.
7. Adam gave him Dominion over the earth.
8. He rules earth and mankind. He roams earth from place to place.
9. He has power to bring storms, pestilence, wars, disease, and death. He can send fire and wind from the heavens.
10. He has access to God to accuse the Church
11. He is to be bound and cast into Hell at Christ's coming
12. At the judgment he is cast into the 'lake of fire', and his reign of terror ends.

RESISTING THE DEVIL
James 4:7 ...*Resist the devil and he will flee from you...*

Here is how you can resist the devil and have daily deliverance from the "devil's D s," all of which can be brought on by a fearful frame of mind.

    1. **Detect** the devil's devices.

    2. **Disagree** with the devil by agreeing with God. Quote the Word because the devil flees at the Name and the Word! That's the reason for this notebook.

        Use the name of Jesus. Mark 16:17 ...*in My name they will cast out demons...*

Boldly quote the Word of God. Rev 12:11 *And they overcame him because of the blood of the Lamb and because of the word of their testimony...*

3. **Defeat.** Rom 8:37 *in all these things we overwhelmingly conquer through Him who loved us...*

4. **Diseases.** Ps 103:3 *Who heals all your diseases*

5. **Discouragement.** Deut 1:21 *...do not fear or be discouraged.* NKJV

6. **Distress.** Rom 8:31 *What then shall we say to these things? If God is for us, who can be against us?* NKJV

7. **Debts.** Phil 4:19 *And my God will supply all your needs...*

8. **Disheartenment** Ps 37:4 *Delight yourself in the Lord; And He will give you the desires of your heart.*

9. **Desolation.** Ps 34:22*...none of them that trust in him shall be desolate.* KJV

10. **Destruction.** John 10:10 *The thief cometh not, but for to steal, and to kill, and to destroy...*KJV

11. **Devouring.** 1 Peter 5:8 *Be of sober spirit, be on the alert. Your adversary, the devil, prowls around like a roaring lion, seeking someone to devour.*

12. **Dishonesty.** 2 Cor 4:2 *But have renounced the hidden things of dishonesty...KJV*

13. **Dissension.** Ps 133:1 *Behold, how good and how pleasant it is for brethren to dwell together in unity!* KJV

14. **Despondency.** Phil 4:4 *Rejoice in the Lord alway: and again I say, Rejoice.* KJV

15. **Doubt.** Acts 27:25*... believe God that it will turn out exactly as I have been told.* Luke 12:29 *And do not seek what you will eat and what you will drink, and do not keep worrying.*

16. **Disappointment.** Rom 8:28*... we know that God causes all things to work together for good to those who love God...*

SLEEP (also see REST)

Ps 127:2 *For so He gives His beloved sleep.* NKJV

Prov 3:24 *Yes, you will lie down and your sleep will be sweet.* NKJV

Ps 17:15 *I shall be satisfied when I awake.* NKJV

Ps 4:8
I will both lie down in peace, and sleep; NKJV

Jer 31:26
I awoke and looked around, and my sleep was sweet to me. NKJV

Isa 63:14 *...the Spirit of the Lord causes him to rest...*NKJV

Matt 8:24 *But He was asleep...* NKJV

Prov 20:13 *Do not love sleep, lest you come to poverty;* NKJV

7 EXAMPLES OF DEEP SLEEP
1. Adam (Gen 2:21).
2. Abraham (Gen 15:12).
3. Saul and his army (1 Sam 26:12).
4. Israel (Isa 29:10).
5. 6. Daniel (8:18; 10:9).
7. Eutychus (Acts 20:9)

Sons of God Now

1 John 3:1 *SEE WHAT [an incredible] quality of love the Father has given (shown, bestowed on) us, that we should [be permitted to] be named and called and counted the children of God!* AMP

John 1:12 *But as many as received Him, to them He gave the right to become children of God, even to those who believe in His name…*

Heb 2:10 *…in bringing many sons to glory.*

2 Cor 6:18 *"And I will be a father to you, And you shall be sons and daughters to Me," Says the Lord Almighty.*

Gal 4:6-7 *Because you are sons, God has sent forth the Spirit of His Son into our hearts, crying, "Abba! Father!"*

Rom 8:16-17 *The Spirit Himself testifies with our spirit that we are children of God, 17 and if children, heirs also, heirs of God and fellow heirs with Christ…*

Rom 8:14-15 *For all who are being led by the Spirit of God, these are sons of God.*

Hos 1:10 *It will be said to them, "You are the sons of the living God."*

Isa 1:2 *For the Lord speaks, "Sons I have reared and brought up…,"*

Be STRONG IN THE LORD

A STUDY

Eph 6:10-11 *...be strong in the Lord and in the strength of His might.*

Josh 1:6 *Be strong and courageous...*

Josh 1:7 *...be strong and very courageous;*

Josh 1:9 *Have I not commanded you? Be strong and courageous!*

Ps 80:2 *Stir up Your strength,* NKJV

2 Chron 15:7 *...be strong and do not let your hands be weak,* NKJV

Ps 71:16 *I will go in the strength of the Lord God;* NKJV

Col 1:11-12 *...strengthened with all might, according to His glorious power, for all patience and longsuffering with joy;* NKJV

Phil 4:13 *I can do all things through Christ who strengthens me.* NKJV

Dan 11:32 *...the people who know their God will display strength and take action.*

Josh 14:11 *I am still as strong today as I was in the day Moses sent me; as my strength was then, so my strength is now...*

2 Sam 3:1 *David grew steadily stronger...*

GOD IS YOUR STRENGTH
Judg 6:14 *"Go in this might of yours..."* NKJV

Isa 26:4 *... in the Lord Jehovah is everlasting strength:* KJV

Ps 27:1 *...the Lord is the strength of my life; of whom shall I be afraid?* KJV

Ps 84:5 *Blessed is the man whose strength is in thee...* KJV

Isa 41:10 *I will strengthen you, surely I will help you...*

Ps 18:1 *"I love You, O Lord, my strength."*

Ps 29:11 *The Lord will give strength to His people;*

TAKE HOLD OF STRENGTH
Isa 27:5 *Or let him take hold of My strength,* NKJV

Isa 52:1 *Put on your strength...* NKJV

Rom 8:31-32
If God is for us, who can be against us? 32 He who did not spare His own Son, but delivered Him up for us all, how shall He not with Him also freely give us all things.
NKJV

1 Cor 2:12-13 *Now we have received, not the spirit of the world, but the Spirit who is from God, so that we may know the things freely given to us by God...*

Mark 11:24 *Therefore I say to you, all things for which you pray and ask, believe that you have received them, and they will be granted you.*

Rev 22:17 *...let the one who wishes take the water of life without cost.*

1 Cor 14:4 *One who speaks in a tongue edifies himself;*

GOD STRENGTHENS THE UPRIGHT
Isa 27:5 *Or let him take hold of My strength...* NKJV

Isa 52:1 *Put on your strength...* NKJV

Rom 8:31-32 *If God is for us, who can be against us? 32 He who did not spare His own Son, but delivered Him up for us all, how shall He not with Him also freely give us all things...* NKJV

1 Cor 2:12-13 *Now we have received, not the spirit of the world, but the Spirit who is from God, so that we may know the things freely given to us by God...*

Mark 11:24 *Therefore I say to you, all things for which you pray and ask, believe that you have received them, and they will be granted you.*

Rev 22:17 *...let the one who wishes take the water of life without cost.*

1 Cor 14:4 *One who speaks in a tongue edifies himself;*

Prov 10:29 *The way of the Lord is a stronghold to the upright...*

Dan 11:32 *...the people who know their God will display strength and take action.*

Ps 68:34-35 *Ascribe strength to God; His majesty is over Israel And His strength is in the skies. 35 O God, You are awesome from Your sanctuary. The God of Israel Himself gives strength and power to the people. Blessed be God!*

Ps 37:39-40 *He is their strength in time of trouble. 40 The Lord helps them and delivers them;*

Prov 24:5 *A wise man is strong...*

Eph 3:16-17 *He would grant you, according to the riches of His glory, to be strengthened with power through His Spirit in the inner man...*

THE WEAK CAN TAKE GOD'S STRENGTH
Joel 3:10 *Let the weak say, "I am a mighty man."*

Isa 40:29 *He gives strength to the weary...*

Isa 33:23 *The lame will take the plunder.*

2 Cor 12:8-10 *And He has said to me, "My grace is sufficient for you, for power is perfected in weakness." Most gladly, therefore, I will rather boast about my weaknesses, so that the power of Christ may dwell in me. 10 Therefore I am well content with weaknesses, with insults, with distresses, with persecutions, with difficulties, for Christ's sake; for when I am weak, then I am strong.*

1 Cor 12:24-25 *...having given greater honor to that part which lacks it...* NKJV

STRENGTH IS RELEASED BY GROWING IN GOD

Ps 27:14 *Wait for the Lord; Be strong and let your heart take courage; Yes, wait for the Lord.*

Ps 84:7 *They go from strength to strength…*

Col 1:11 *…strengthened with all power, according to His glorious might…*

THE JOY OF THE LORD IS MY STRENGTH
Neh 8:10 *… the joy of the Lord is your strength…*

Ps 5:11 *But let all who take refuge in You be glad, Let them ever sing for joy;*

STRENGTH IS SHORT CIRCUITED BY SIN
Ps 31:10 *For my life is spent with sorrow And my years with sighing; My strength has failed because of my iniquity, And my body has wasted away.*

Stumbling

1 John 2:9-11 *He who loves his brother abides in the light, and there is no cause for stumbling in him.* NKJV

2 Peter 1:10 *Therefore, brethren, be even more diligent to make your call and election sure, for if you do these things you will never stumble;* NKJV

Prov 3:23 *Then you will walk safely in your way, And your foot will not stumble.* NKJV

Mark 4:16-18 *These likewise are the ones sown on stony ground who, when they hear the word, immediately receive it with gladness; 17 and they have no root in themselves, and so endure only for a time. Afterward, when tribulation or persecution arises for the word's sake, immediately they stumble.* NKJV

Rom 14:21 *It is good neither to eat meat nor drink wine nor do anything by which your brother stumbles or is offended or is made weak.* NKJV

Prov 4:12 *When you walk, your steps will not be hindered, And when you run, you will not stumble.* NKJV

Ps 27:2 *When the wicked came against me To eat up my flesh, My enemies and foes, They stumbled and fell.* NKJV

Jude 24-25 *Now to Him who is able to keep you from stumbling, And to present you faultless Before the presence of His glory with exceeding joy, 25 To God our Savior.* NKJV

Jer 31:9 *They shall come with weeping, And with supplications I will lead them. I will cause them to walk by the rivers of waters, In a straight way in which they shall not stumble;* NKJV

TRIALS AND AFFLICTIONS

A STUDY

Ps 107:17 *Fools, because of their rebellious way, And because of their iniquities, were afflicted.*

Ps 25:18-20 *Look upon my affliction and my trouble, And forgive all my sins. 19 Look upon my enemies, for they are many, And they hate me with violent hatred. 20 Guard my soul and deliver me;*

Col 1:24 *Now I rejoice in my sufferings for your sake.*

2 Cor 1:5 *For just as the sufferings of Christ are ours in abundance, so also our comfort is abundant through Christ.*

1 Peter 4:13-14 *...but to the degree that you share the sufferings of Christ, keep on rejoicing, so that also at the revelation of His glory you may rejoice with exultation.*

Ps 119:75 *I know, O Lord, that Your judgments are righteous, And that in faithfulness You have afflicted me.*

Lam 3:33 *For He does not afflict willingly Or grieve the sons of men.*

Ps 34:19 *Many are the afflictions of the righteous, But the Lord delivers him out of them all.*

Isa 48:10 *Behold, I have refined you, but not as silver; I have tested you in the furnace of affliction.*

2 Cor 2:4 *For out of much affliction and anguish of heart I wrote to you with many tears; not so that you would be made sorrowful, but that you might know the love which I have especially for you.*

2 Cor 4:17 *For momentary, light affliction is producing for us an eternal weight of glory far beyond all comparison,*

Ps 119:71 *It is good for me that I was afflicted, That I may learn Your statutes.*

1 Peter 1:6-7 *In this you greatly rejoice, even though now for a little while, if necessary, you have been distressed by various trials, 7 so that the proof of your faith, being more precious than gold which is perishable, even though tested by fire, may be found to result in praise and glory and honor at the revelation of Jesus Christ;*

Ps 34:19 *Many are the afflictions of the righteous, But the Lord delivers him out of them all.*

Isa 48:10 *Behold, I have refined you, but not as silver; I have tested you in the furnace of affliction.*

2 Cor 2:4 *For out of much affliction and anguish of heart I wrote to you with many tears;*

Mark 4:17 *...they have no firm root in themselves, but are only temporary; then, when affliction or persecution arises because of the word, immediately they fall away.*

Ps 119:71 *It is good for me that I was afflicted, That I may learn Your statutes.*

1 Peter 1:6-7 *In this you greatly rejoice, even though now for a little while, if necessary, you have been distressed by various trials, 7 so that the proof of your faith, being more precious than gold which is perishable, even though tested by fire, may be found to result in praise and glory and honor at the revelation of Jesus Christ*

James 5:13 *Is anyone among you suffering? Then he must pray*

Jonah 2:2 *I called out of my distress to the Lord, And He answered me.*

Affliction in Hebrew is "ra" meaning bad, calamity, sorrow, or grief. It never means sickness. It results from sowing and reaping.

ELEVEN CAUSES OF AFFLICTION

1. Sin (Gen 3:16)

7. Mistreatment of others (Gen 27:1-46 and 32:1)

2. Backsliding (Ps 119:67)
3. Misuse of tongue (Pro 26:28)
4. Resentment (Gen 16:4-11)
5. Pride (Job 33-14-29)
6. Impenitence (Pro 1:30-31)
8. Hardness of heart (Judg 10:6-10)
9. Idolatry (Judg 10:6-10)
10. Forgetting God (1 Sam 12:9-10)
11. Hypocrisy (Matt 23)

TEN PROMISES IN AFFLICTION. GOD WILL:
1. Hear the afflicted (Job 34:28)
2. Save (Ps 18:27)
3. Have mercy (Isa 49:13)
4. Deliver from fear (Ps 23:4)
5. Deliver out of troubles (Ps 34:19; 50:15)
6. Uphold (Ps 37:23:33)
7. Reward (Matt 5:10-12)
8. Be a refuge (Ps 9:9-10)
9. Hide one (Ps 27:5)
10. Give enough grace
(2 Cor 12:9)

SEVEN WAYS A PERSON CAN BE AFFLICTED
1. Oppression (Gen 15:13; Ex 1:11-12)
2. Hardships of various kinds (James 1:27; Heb 12:5; Ex 22:22-23)
3. Family troubles (Gen 16:1-11)
4. Barrenness (1 Sam 1:11)
5. Imprisonment (Ps 107:10)
6. Persecution (2 Cor 2:4; Mark 13:19)
7. Poverty and hunger (Ruth 1:21; Ps 107:38-41)

TRUTH

Deut 32:4 *He is the Rock, His work is perfect; For all His ways are justice, A God of truth and without injustice; Righteous and upright is He.* NKJV

Ps 31:5 *Into Your hand I commit my spirit; You have redeemed me, O Lord God of truth.* NKJV

Isa 65:16 *So that he who blesses himself in the earth Shall bless himself in the God of truth;* NKJV

John 1:14 *And the Word became flesh and dwelt among us, and we beheld His glory, the glory as of the only begotten of the Father, full of grace and truth.* NKJV

John 15:26 *But when the Helper comes, whom I shall send to you from the Father, the Spirit of truth who proceeds from the Father...* NKJV

John 16:13 *...when He, the Spirit of truth, has come, He will guide you into all truth;* NKJV

1 John 5:6 *...it is the Spirit who bears witness, because the Spirit is truth.* NKJV

Prov 6:16-17 *...the Lord hates...17...A lying tongue...* NKJV

Prov 12:22 *Lying lips are an abomination to the Lord...* NKJV

Zech 8:16 *These are the things you shall do: Speak each man the truth to his neighbor; Give judgment in your gates for truth, justice, and peace;* NKJV

Eph 4:25 *Therefore, putting away lying, "Let each one of you speak truth with his neighbor,"* NKJV

Eph 4:15 *...but, speaking the truth in love...* NKJV

WAIT IN GOD

Ps 62:1 *Truly my soul silently waits for God;* NKJV

Ps 25:5 *...I wait all the day.* NKJV

Ps 27:14 *Wait on the Lord; Be of good courage, And He shall strengthen your heart; Wait, I say, on the Lord!* NKJV

Ps 37:7 Rest in the Lord, and wait patiently for Him; NKJV

Ps 37:34 *Wait on the Lord, And keep His way.* NKJV

Ps 130:5-6 *I wait for the Lord, my soul waits, And in His word I do hope. 6 My soul waits for the Lord...* NKJV

Prov 20:22 *Wait for the Lord, and He will save you.* NKJV

Isa 8:17 *And I will wait on the Lord, Who hides His face from the house...* NKJV

Isa 30:18 *Therefore the Lord will wait, that He may be gracious to you;* NKJV

Isa 40:31 *But those who wait on the Lord Shall renew their strength;* NKJV

Lam 3:25-26 *The Lord is good to those who wait for Him, To the soul who seeks Him. 26 It is good that one should hope and wait quietly For the salvation of the Lord.* NKJV

Hos 12:6 *...wait on your God continually.* NKJV

Gal 5:5-6 *For we through the Spirit eagerly wait for the hope of righteousness by faith.* NKJV

TWENTY-ONE REASONS TO WAIT IN GOD

1. Freedom from shame (Ps 25:3)
2. Integrity and uprightness (Ps 25:21)
12. Salvation (Ps 62:1; Rom 8"35)
13. Daily supply (Ps 104:27-28)

3. Preservation (25:21)	14. Counsel (Ps 106:13)
4. Renewed strength and courage (Ps 27:14; Isa 40:31)	
5. Life (Ps 33:19:20)	15. Revelation pf Gpd (Isa 25:9
6. Help and protection (Ps 33:20)	16. Justice (Isa 26:8-9)
7. Mercy (Ps 33:22)	17. Blessing (Isa 30:19)
8. Patience (Ps 37:7-9)	18. Eternal things (Isa 647:4)
9. Inheritance of the earth (Ps 37:34)	19. Goodness of God (Lam 3:25)
10. Hope (Ps 37:7-8; Gal 5:5) Acts 1:4)	20. Holy Spirit baptism (Luke 24:49;
11. Answers to prayer (Ps 40:1-3) 1:7)	21. Second advent (Luke 12:36; 1 Cor

SEVEN WAYS OF WAITING IN GOD

1. Prayerfully (Ps 25:4-5)	5. Longingly (Ps 130:5-6)
2. Patiently (Ps 37:7; 145:15)	6. Quietly (Lam 3:26)
3. Single-mindedly (Ps 62:5)	7. Continually (Hos 12:60)
4. Expectantly (Ps 62:5-6; Mic 7:7)	

SEVEN EXAMPLES OF WAITING ON GOD

1. Jacob (Gen 49:18)	5. Micah (7:7)
2. David (Ps 25:4-5; 33:18-22)	6. Simeon (Luke 2:25)
3. Isaiah (8:17)	7. All creation (Ps 104:25-28)
4. Jeremiah (14:22)	

PATIENCE

Luke 8:15 *...these are the ones who have heard the word in an honest and good heart, and hold it fast, and bear fruit with perseverance.*

Heb 10:36 *...or you have need of endurance, so that when you have done the will of God, you may receive what was promised.*

Heb 10:23 *Let us hold fast the confession of our hope without wavering,*

Heb 6:12 *...so that you will not be sluggish, but imitators of those who through faith and patience inherit the promises.*

James 1:4 *But let patience have its perfect work...* NKJV

Luke 21:19 *By your patience possess your souls...* NKJV

Rom 15:4-5 *For whatever was written in earlier times was written for our instruction, so that through perseverance and the encouragement of the Scriptures we might have hope.*

Rom 5:4 *And endurance (fortitude) develops maturity of character (approved faith and tried integrity).* AMP

Rom 8:25 *...with perseverance we wait eagerly for it.*

Ex 23:30 *I will drive them out before you little by little, until you become fruitful and take possession of the land.*

WHO AM I?

A DECLARATION

When you need confidence in your place in life, you can know exactly who you are once you make Christ your Lord. This was written by the author many years ago, and is still a profession of Truth from the Scriptures.

"I am a new creature in Christ Jesus. Yes, I am.
What does this mean? It means that the moment I received Christ as my personal Savior and Lord, I was born into God's royal family. I am a son of God. God has created me now in Christ Jesus. He has put new life into me. I have been born from above, born of the Spirit. Every thing that God creates is good. I will not run down my life, because my life is in Christ. He has made me to be... **A** New Creature. I will not belittle myself, for I am in Christ, and in Christ, I have been granted new life. The old life is gone, I am a citizen of a new kingdom. My citizenship is in Heaven.

"If you see an angel, ask him and he will tell you that my name is written down in Heaven. O wonder of wonders, I am a new creation in Christ. Created by God, His own workmanship. God is now working within me both to will and do of His own good pleasure. What is God doing with me? He is building me up! Making me strong in faith. How is He doing this? By His own Word!

"I am the righteousness of God in Christ. How do I know this? 2 Corinthians 5:21 is one of the great statements, among others, that tells me this fact. I am now righteous in Christ. Not only a new creature in Christ, but righteous in Christ. What does it mean to be righteous? It means that I possess the divine ability to be able to stand in God's holy presence without any sense of unworthiness. It means that God has made me righteous with His own righteousness. I stand before Him with no sense of. unworthiness. So now that I am complete in Christ, I am free from that old inferiority complex that once held me captive.

"I am redeemed from the kingdom of darkness and I have been translated into the Kingdom of God's dear Son. Once I was held in the realm of spiritual darkness. Satan was my lord and master. I was chained, bound, doomed for eternity in Hell. But then Jesus came and broke the bonds, loosed my soul from eternal damnation and gave me His life. I am now in that great kingdom where He reigns as Lord of lords and King of kings. He invites me to join Him right on the Throne. I reign with Him in life. Yes, I am redeemed. Once I lived in awful bondage to Satan. Sin was my master. I lived to gratify the flesh. But now in this new kingdom, sin has no dominion over me. In the old kingdom of darkness, I lived under the sway of sickness, fear, poverty, and failure. I was held by unclean powers. But now through the blood of Jesus, I have been delivered. I say it boldly, 'Goodbye sickness, goodbye fear, goodbye lack, goodbye weakness. I am free!' Now I live in a new kingdom the heavenly kingdom where there is life, light, liberty, joy, peace, health, assurance, blessing and power.

"What a redemption is mine! What a Redeemer I have!

"I am an heir of God and a joint heir with Jesus Christ. To be saved isn't a light thing, I have received a rich inheritance. I am blessed with every spiritual blessing in the heavenly places in Christ Jesus. My Father loves me as He loved the Lord Jesus. My own wonderful Father is greater than all. He loves me with an everlasting
love. Yes, I am blessed with heaven's best.

"My Christ said, 'I am the vine and ye are the branches.' That's how close I am linked with Him. He's that living Vine and I am a branch of that Vine. That same life, love, joy, peace, power, wisdom, and ability that flows in the Vine flows into the branch. Wherever I, the branch go, the Vine-life flows!

"I have the life of God in my mortal body right now. Not just when I get to heaven, but now, my spirit has been quickened, made alive and now I live and move and have my being in Christ. I have what God says I have. I can do what God says I can do. I am what God says I am.

"I (insert your name) affirm that the above facts are forever settled in Heaven and are now settled in my heart. I shall often speak them boldly and possess my possessions in Christ Jesus. This is who I am."

Wisdom

A STUDY

Ps 37:30-31 *The mouth of the righteous utters wisdom, And his tongue speaks justice. 31 The law of his God is in his heart;*

Ex 28:3 *You shall speak to all the skillful persons whom I have endowed with the spirit of wisdom.*

James 1:5 *But if any of you lacks wisdom, let him ask of God, who gives to all generously and without reproach, and it will be given to him.*

James 3:13 *Who among you is wise and understanding? Let him show by his good behavior his deeds in the gentleness of wisdom.*

> **James 3:14-16 lists eight characteristics of *fake* wisdom:** *Bitter, strife, glory in self, having only this life in view, sensual, devilish, confusion, and evil.*
>
> **James 3:17 lists eight characteristics of *divine* wisdom:** *Pure, peaceable, gentle, not stubborn, full of mercy, full of good fruits, without partiality, and honest.*

Prov 2:6-7 *For the Lord gives wisdom; From His mouth come knowledge and understanding. 7 He stores up sound wisdom for the upright;*

Prov 3:13 *How blessed is the man who finds wisdom And the man who gains understanding.*

Prov 4:5-8 *Acquire wisdom! Acquire understanding! Do not forget nor turn away from the words of my mouth. 6 "Do not forsake her, and she will guard you; Love her, and she will watch over you. 7 "The beginning of wisdom is: Acquire wisdom; And with all your acquiring, get understanding. 8 "Prize her, and she will exalt you; She will honor you if you embrace her."*

Prov 8:17 *And those who diligently seek me will find me* (wisdom).

2 Tim 2:7 *Consider what I say, for the Lord will give you understanding in everything.*

FIVE PERSONS WHO RECEIVED WISDOM

1. Joseph (Gen 41:38-39)
2. Moses (Ex 4:12)
3. Solomon (1 Kings 3:12; 4:29)
4. Daniel (1:17; 2:23)
5. Stephen (Acts 6:5; 10)

Wisdom is

...*better than strength* (Eccl 9:16)

...*better than weapons* (Eccl 9:18)

...*better than rubies* (Pro 8:11)

THANK GOD FOR HIS

The WORD

Each of us can say this in thanksgiving for the living Word of God:

David said, "Your word I have treasured in my heart, That I may not sin against You." Ps 119:11

Again, in Ps 119:130 "The entrance of Your words gives light; It gives understanding to the simple." NKJV

And then in Ps 119:89 "Forever, O Lord, Your word is settled in heaven."

The Lord said through Jeremiah: "Behold, I have put My words in your mouth." (1:9) *and later* "Your words were found and I ate them, And Your words became for me a joy and the delight of my heart" (15:16)

God told Ezekiel to take the roll of writings and eat them
"Son of man, eat what you find; eat this scroll, and go, speak to the house of Israel." 2 So I opened my mouth, and He fed me this scroll. 3 He said to me, "Son of man, feed your stomach and fill your body with this scroll which I am giving you." Then I ate it, and it was sweet as honey in my mouth. (Ezek 3:1-3) AMP

He told Isaiah to "Seek out of the book of the Lord and read..." (Isa 34:16) AMP

Then, Paul said, "For the Word that God speaks is alive and full of power..." (Heb 4:12) AMP *and* "Be diligent to present yourself approved to God as a workman who does not need to be ashamed, accurately handling the word of truth." (2 Tim 2:15). He also said "...by the washing of water with the word" (Eph 5:26"

And Peter said, "BUT THE WORD OF THE LORD ENDURES FOREVER." (1 Peter 1:25)

The Importance of the

WORDS YOU SPEAK

A STUDY

The words you speak, or release, are extremely important. God, in His creation, with all the variety of animals and fish, chose to give humans the ability to say words. *You were made to be quite special.* He created everything by using words as containers to carry His power and then gave man the same vehicle to use. The words that you speak affect others, but just as importantly, affect yourself. You hear your words, directly and indirectly, a double dose of your own words. The words you say help to build yourself up or break yourself down. Simple things like negative words such as "I'll never reach that goal," "My children are no good," or "I'm going to be sick" affect your mind and heart (spirit). Why not turn them around and believe the positive side "J can do that," "I refuse to lose," or "I'm not going to be sick, I'm full of health," "My children *are* great." Now, the words themselves do not create! However, they do two important things. One, they build up or tear down, and two, they carry faith or fear to help create the result. Do not allow this study to get "out of balance" as many have. It is a subject that needs to be understood. It is true and powerful, but do not abuse it or use it in the wrong way. Confession or good words or even confession of God's Words by itself, is not a formula to force God into doing something. All your words   must be ruled by love and prayer.

Read the many scriptures which follow. They summarize the importance of the word you speak. Then watch what you say, and work towards releasing only a vehicle which builds up! Isa 45:24 (AMP) *Only in the Lord shall one say, I have righteousness, salvation and victory, and strength to achieve.* Ps 118:28 *You are my God and I will confess, praise and give thanks to you.*

James 1:26-27 *If anyone thinks himself to be religious, and yet does not bridle his tongue but deceives his own heart, this man's religion is worthless.*

1 Peter 3:10 *THE ONE WHO DESIRES LIFE, TO LOVE AND SEE GOOD DAYS, MUST KEEP HIS TONGUE FROM EVIL AND HIS LIPS FROM SPEAKING DECEIT.*

Prov 15:4 *A soothing tongue is a tree of life, But perversion in it crushes the spirit.*

Ps 141:3 *Set a guard, O Lord, over my mouth; Keep watch over the door of my lips.*

Prov 16:24 *Pleasant words are a honeycomb, Sweet to the soul and healing to the bones.*

Prov 10:19-20 *When there are many words, transgression is unavoidable, But he who restrains his lips is wise. 20 The tongue of the righteous is as choice silver...*

Prov 10:21 *The lips of the righteous feed many...*

Luke 21:15 *...for I will give you a mouth and wisdom which all your adversaries will not be able to contradict or resist.* NKJV

Prov 21:23 *Whoever guards his mouth and tongue Keeps his soul from troubles.* NKJV

Eph 4:29 *Let no corrupt word proceed out of your mouth, but what is good for necessary edification, that it may impart grace to the hearers.* NKJV

Prov 18:21 *Death and life are in the power of the tongue, And those who love it will eat its fruit.* NKJV

Prov 6:2 *You are snared by the words of your mouth; You are taken by the words of your mouth.* NKJV

Prov 12:13-14 *The wicked is ensnared by the transgression of his lips, But the righteous will come through trouble. 14 A man will be satisfied with good by the fruit of his mouth, And the recompense of a man's hands will be rendered to him.* NKJV

Prov 12:18-19 *There is one who speaks like the piercings of a sword, But the tongue of the wise promotes health. 19 The truthful lip shall be established forever, But a lying tongue is but for a moment.* NKJV

Hos 14:2 *Take words with you, And return to the Lord. Say to Him...* NKJV

Isa 57:19 *I create the fruit of the lips...* NKJV

Rom 10:10 *For with the heart one believes unto righteousness, and with the mouth confession is made unto salvation.* NKJV

Matt 12:36-37 *But I say to you that for every idle word men may speak, they will give account of it in the day of judgment.   37 For by your words you will be justified, and by your words you will be condemned.* NKJV

Prov 15:23 *A man has joy by the answer of his mouth, And a word spoken in due season, how good it is!* NKJV

Prov 10:11 *The mouth of the righteous is a well of life, But violence covers the mouth of the wicked.* NKJV

Many people have difficulty expressing or professing something they do not actually see with their eyes. They think that perhaps it is a lie. Keep in mind two scriptures as you study this topic: 1. Heb 11:1-2 *Now faith is the substance of things hoped for, the evidence of things not seen* NKJV; 2. Rom 4:17 *...God, who gives life to the dead and calls those things which do not exist as though they did.* NKJV.

A good principle to start with is simply agreeing with what God (who cannot lie) says. We cannot lie when we simply say what God says.

WE ARE WHO GOD SAYS WE ARE
1. We are new creatures, a new species of man that has never been in existence 2 Cor 5:17 *Therefore if any person is [ingrafted] in Christ (the Messiah) he is a new creation (a new creature altogether); the old [previous moral and spiritual condition] has passed away. Behold, the fresh and new has come.* AMP

2. Col 1:13 *He has delivered us from the power of darkness and conveyed us into the kingdom of the Son of His love.* NKJV

3. Rom 8:37 *Yet in all these things we are more than conquerors through Him who loved us.* NKJV

4. Rom 8:17 *if children, heirs also, heirs of God and fellow heirs with Christ,*

5. Eph 1:3 *who has blessed us with every spiritual blessing in the heavenly places in Christ,* NASU

253

WE HAVE WHAT GOD SAYS WE HAVE

1. We have abundance of full life, 1 John 5:12-13 *He who has the Son has life; he who does not have the Son of God does not have life.* NKJV

2. We have light, John 8:12 *He who follows Me shall not walk in darkness, but have the light of life.* NKJV

3. We have liberty, 2 Cor 3:17-18 *Now the Lord is the Spirit; and where the Spirit of the Lord is, there is liberty.* NKJV

4. We have love, Rom 5:5...*the love of God has been poured out in our hearts.* NKJV

5. We have joy, John 16:22 ...*your heart will rejoice, and your joy no one will take from you.* NKJV

6. We have pardon, 1 John 1:7...*the blood of Jesus Christ His Son cleanses us from all sin.* NKJV

7. We have peace, Rom 5:1-2...*we have peace with God through our Lord Jesus Christ,* NKJV

8. We have purpose, Phil 1:21 *For to me, to live is Christ,* NKJV

9. We have power, Acts 1:8 *But you shall receive power when the Holy Spirit has come upon you.* NKJV

10. We have provision, Phil 4:19 *And my God shall supply all your need...*NKJV

11. We have prospect John 14:2-3 *In My Father's house are many mansions; if it were not so, I would have told you. I go to prepare a place for you.* NKJV

WE CAN DO WHAT GOD SAYS WE CAN DO

Phil 4:13 *I can do all things through Christ who strengthens me.* NKJV

WORSHIP

Matt 4:10 *...worship the Lord your God, and Him alone shall you serve.* AMP

Worship and praise are the crown jewels of your life in Christ. Chose the way you worship God, the way you are most comfortable with. (See PRAISE and WAIT in this book).

- **We can do it bowing:** *Come, let us worship and bow down...* (Ps 95:6a)

- **We can do it kneeling:** *Let us kneel before the Lord our Maker.* (Ps 95:6b)

- **We can do it standing:** *My foot stands on a level place; In the congregations I shall bless the Lord.* (Ps 26:12)

- **We can do it with lifted hands:** *I desire therefore that in every place men should pray, without anger or quarreling or resentment or doubt [in their minds], lifting up holy hands.* (1 Tim 2:8 AMP)

- **We can do it by clapping our hands:** *O clap your hands, all peoples; Shout to God with the voice of joy.* (Ps 47:1)

- **We can do it with our feet:** *Let them praise His name with dancing;* (Ps 149:3)

NOTES

AUTHOR

Thomas Hiegel has served as a highly respected pastor, teacher, financial director, and administrator. Now retired, he has authored five previously published books, and several sought after Manuscripts/research papers such as "From the Cross to the Throne" and "The Nephilim." Currently, he is writing a history of the *Bible Lands, Cities, and Peoples*. His "Pre-History" on the origin of the cities of Mesopotamia is unique and will be in great demand by history "buffs." He also will be releasing his long-awaited theology work *The Essence of Christian Belief.*

Thomas is happily married and is deeply devoted to his best friend, life-long partner, and wife...Sandy. He has one daughter, Michele, and two grandsons, Spencer and Simon. His home is near Dayton, Ohio.

www.ingramcontent.com/pod-product-compliance
Lightning Source LLC
Chambersburg PA
CBHW071415090426
42737CB00011B/1477